BOAT HANDLING

UNDER SAIL & POWER

BOAT HANDLING

UNDER SAIL & POWER

Tom Cunliffe
and
Bill Anderson

fernhurst
BOOKS

First published in 1995 by Fernhurst Books, Duke's Path,High Street,
Arundel, West Sussex, BN18 9AJ, UK

Printed and bound in Great Britain

British Library Cataloguing in Publication Data:
A catalogue record for this book is available from the British
Library.

ISBN 1 898 660 15 8

Acknowledgments

The authors and publishers would like to thank the Buckley family for the
loan of their Jeanneau 28 *Equity* for the photo sessions, and Annie Buckley,
Simon Davison, Bill Anderson and Peter Milne for crewing her.

Cover photo by Crystal Clear, courtesy of the RYA.
All other photos by Chris Davies and Tom Cunliffe.

Edited by Jeremy Evans
DTP by Creative Byte, Bournemouth
Cover design by Simon Balley
Printed and bound by Ebenezer Baylis & Son, Worcester
Text set in 10PT Rockwell Light

Contents

INTRODUCTION

When contemplating our qualifications to write a book on boat handling, we decided that our best platform was to advise readers, hand-on-heart, that we shall in all probability earn less from the royalties on this work than we have spent making good the results of our own less successful manoeuvres over the years.

It is always dangerous to shout the odds about the 'right' and 'wrong' way to tackle any facet of seafaring, and boat handling is no exception. For this reason, no sensible sailing organisation has ever proposed a 'method' for doing anything aboard a cruiser. The fact that we are both deeply involved with the RYA should therefore emphatically not be taken to mean that any words of wisdom (or otherwise) found in this book are 'The Word'. We are two long-term boat operators passing on lessons learned from our own mistakes. That is all.

You might be excused for imagining that because one of us sails a 35 ton gaff cutter and the other a 24ft light displacement flyer, we would have irreconcilable views on all subjects maritime. Surprisingly, we have agreed on every important proposition in this book. To be successful, boat handling requires experience, which is not for sale. Fortunately, even the oldest hands still base their judgements on the principles of seamanship. Understand these, and you are more than halfway there.

In this book we have isolated some of the elements of sound boat handling, so that the reader may literally take them on board and use them in the day-to-day running of their yacht - sailors who know what to look for as a situation arises will enjoy a far smoother passage up the learning curve.

The book has not only been pitched to provide a primer for the novice, but also to be of real value to yachtsmen who know they still have room for improvement. Use it retrospectively, as well as before going sailing. The constructive analysis of every manoeuvre, successful or untidy, is the surest path to steady development.

Tom Cunliffe and Bill Anderson.

1 Knowing Boat, Wind and Water

Watch a really good helmsman sailing to windward through a crowded area of moorings. He makes it look easy. There is no significant weight on the wheel or tiller, and there appear to be so few obstacles in his path that he could be sailing through an empty area of sea.

There are two fundamental reasons for his dexterity. First, he never uses the helm to force the boat to do anything that she can not manage naturally under the influence of the wind on the sails and the water on her hull. Secondly, he is keeping a close eye on everything around him, planning his tacks in advance and anticipating windshifts, as well as changes in strength and direction of the tidal stream.

Honing these skills to perfection takes years of experience, but the rudiments can be acquired relatively quickly. The secret of success is to know your boat, understand how she reacts to the breeze, and observe the clues which indicate changes in wind and tidal stream. The way to learn a boat's handling characteristics is not just to sail her on passages, but to put her through a carefully considered series of manoeuvres. These will indicate her natural reactions when left to her own devices, what she can be made to do, and what she will not countenance at any price.

BOAT HANDLING UNDER POWER

The pivot point

Unlike a road vehicle, which steers by turning a pair of wheels at its forward extremity, a boat swivels around a loosely defined pivoting point in the vicinity of her keel. Thus, when the helm is put over, the stern swings one way and the bow the other, with the overall result that the vessel turns. This fact is irrelevant to course alterations made on passage, but vital in close-up boat handling. For example, if you attempt to steer directly off a dock you will fail. The stern tries to swing in, the dock wall stops it, and as a result the bow cannot turn out. To overcome the problem, it is necessary somehow to force the bows away from the dock. There are a number of ways of achieving this, including a good shove. They will be dealt with later in the book, but it is important that the basic proposition is understood from the outset.

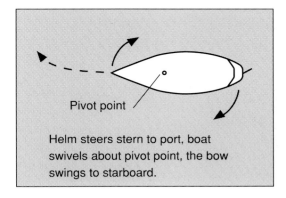

Pivot point

Helm steers stern to port, boat swivels about pivot point, the bow swings to starboard.

Bare poles

Choose a day with a moderate breeze, select an empty patch of flat sea, and start by finding out how the boat settles with the engine stopped and no sail set. Most lie within 20° of beam-on to the wind. Those with long keels normally take up a fairly constant angle, while yachts with short fins or bilge keels tend to veer about.

How fast is the boat drifting sideways? A vessel's performance in this respect to a certain extent parallels the behaviour just described for different keel configurations. The drift rate is generally slow for a long-keel yacht, because lateral resistance is maintained at very low speeds or when the boat is stopped. Short fins only function efficiently when there is water flowing past them, sliding rapidly sideways when the boat is moving slowly or making no way at all.

When you have satisfied yourself about these fundamentals, put the engine into gear, point directly downwind, then take off the power. How long can you maintain steerage within about 30 degrees of directly downwind? In winds of Force 4 or above, most boats will run to leeward under bare poles with reasonable control, making sufficient way to steer comfortably. With Force 5 in flat water, some vessels will pick up considerable momentum and carry it far enough to be sailed through a full circle. This can be a useful attribute if you lose the engine in a tight spot, because the simplest way out of this nightmare may well be to keep going under the windage of your rig while sorting out a plan of action.

Propeller effect

Most boats are prone to a certain amount of 'paddle-wheel effect' or 'prop-walk', causing the stern to kick out when the

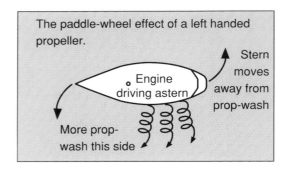

The paddle-wheel effect of a left handed propeller.

Engine driving astern

Stern moves away from prop-wash

More prop-wash this side

engine is put ahead or astern. It is crucial to know which way this will be.

With a right-handed propeller (turning clockwise going ahead when viewed from astern) the stern will kick to starboard when the engine is put ahead, and to port when astern propulsion is engaged. One explanation of this phenomenon is that the lower blade is working in denser water, and therefore acts like a paddle-wheel moving the stern sideways. Although probably flawed, this is a convenient myth, because as long as you know which way the propeller rotates you are in a position to predict the direction in which it will throw the stern. The extent of this effect varies considerably from boat to boat, but it is always more noticeable when the engine is going astern than when it is going ahead. A little experimentation, preferably on a calm day, will soon tell you the side she favours, and whether or not it is a dominant factor in your boat's handling characteristics.

There are two means of sorting out your prop-walk. The first is to motor slowly ahead, take the engine out of gear, then run it half astern with the boat still carrying headway. After a few seconds she will start to swing to one side or the other as the propeller takes hold. This effect will be consistent, and once determined you will always know which way the boat's head wants to look when you run the engine

Tie up firmly, then run the engine astern. One side of the boat may have more prop-wash than the other.

astern, even if you cannot remember whether your propeller is right or left-handed. The second method is to run your engine astern while tied securely to a dock. If she is prone to prop-walk, you will observe much more prop-wash welling up under one quarter. In a free-floating situation she would try to move her stern away from the side with the greater prop-wash, so that is the way she is going to swing her aft end.

Effects of windage under way

One reason for trying out propeller effects in a light breeze, is that the combined effects of windage and hull shape can be equally significant in determining a boat's power-handling characteristics under a given set of circumstances. Motor 'half ahead' in a beam wind and let go of the tiller. It is probable that the boat will slowly round up head to wind and keep going that way. Now stop the boat beam on to the wind. Run the engine astern and try to steer in a straight line. As she starts to gather way you are unlikely to succeed. Subject always to propeller effects, the stern will seek the wind, and at least initially no amount of rudder will stop her. As speed builds up the rudder can begin to overcome the propeller and the wind, bringing the boat under better control and allowing you to steer in any direction. The reason for this wind-seeking tendency is the shifting of the pivot point of the hull when the boat is in motion ahead or astern. Going ahead the pivot point is displaced forward; going astern it moves aft. The extent of this phenomenon varies considerably from boat to boat, so experimenting is the only way to find out how it affects yours.

Some yachts, particularly those with long keels, are virtually impossible to steer astern. Control is marginal in a flat calm, and in any wind at all the stern flies up into the wind so that nothing you can do with the rudder will hold her straight. Such craft are also frequently prone to extremely positive prop-walk. Both this and the desire of the stern to look up to the breeze are entirely predictable, even though they may be beyond your control. It is therefore untrue to say of a boat, "You never know what she'll do astern...". The important thing is to foretell her predilections, and if these are going to be unacceptable, don't give her the opportunity to indulge them. Good boat handlers do not place yachts in predicaments where their only exit is barred by their vessel's natural tendencies. They go somewhere else instead.

Applying the brakes

Since boats have no brakes, the only way of actively stopping one under power is to run the engine astern. Unfortunately, most fixed propellers are less efficient in this mode than when driving ahead. To determine how well your boat can manage the job, try motoring past a buoy at various speeds. As it comes abeam, engage astern gear and see how far the boat travels before she stops. Note also to what extent prop-walk is throwing her around; when you are trying to lose way with little space for manoeuvre,

it can be helpful to correct any tendency to sheer to one side before it happens.

Repeat this exercise using different levels of power. You may find that a fistful of throttle is actually less effective than a gentler approach because the propeller cavitates at high revolutions astern, whereas at lower power it seems to exert a better grip on the water.

Slow speed propeller and rudder control

The main question here is how slowly you can motor and still maintain control, particularly head-to-wind. Most boats have a critical speed below which it is impossible to hold them directly into the wind. Drop below this and the bow is simply blown sideways. The stronger the wind, the higher the minimum speed will be.

Most yachts have their rudders mounted immediately abaft the propeller. This is advantageous because at slow speeds a short, solid burst of power ahead will often kick a boat back into line before it starts to accelerate her to any appreciable extent. The rudder works by diverting the water flowing past it. Most of the time this flow is created by the boat moving through the water, but the slipstream from the

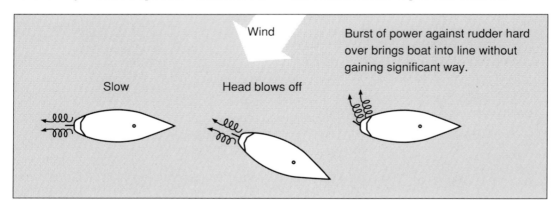

Wind

Burst of power against rudder hard over brings boat into line without gaining significant way.

Slow   Head blows off

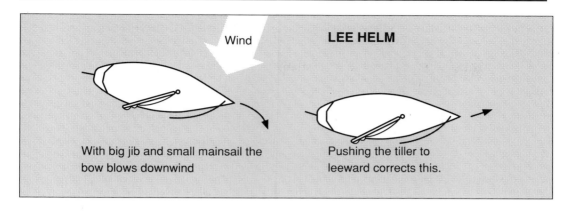

With big jib and small mainsail the bow blows downwind

LEE HELM

Pushing the tiller to leeward corrects this.

propeller can generate the same effect. Once again, an experiment will determine at how slow a speed you can hold your boat head-to-wind by using bursts of power against the rudder. Remember that when the engine is running astern, the propeller is not directing a water stream over the rudder, so the only slow speed assistance available is from the uni-directional prop-walk.

BOAT HANDLING UNDER SAIL

Balance

The mysteries of this apparently difficult art are all locked up in the concept of balance. The classic explanation of balance under sail is based on the relative positions of the centre of effort (CE) of the rig and the centre of lateral resistance (CLR) about which the hull pivots. If the CE is forward of

WEATHER HELM

Big mainsail and small jib make the boat try to round up. Tiller pulled to windward (or weather) counteracts this tendency.

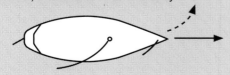

the CLR, the boat will try to turn away from the wind pivoting around her CLR. This is corrected by pushing the tiller to leeward, or steering the boat up to windward with a wheel. Such a tendency is known as 'lee helm'. If the CE falls abaft the CLR, the opposite effect will be experienced i.e. 'weather helm'.

The above explanation only tells half the truth about balance, because it considers a static situation whereas there are in addition many influential dynamic effects. Like the 'paddle-wheel' theory it produces a convenient myth which provides the most practical single guide to achieving a balanced yacht. Setting a larger headsail and reefing the mainsail in order to move the CE forward will help to reduce weather helm in an almost stationary vessel, but other factors such as angle of heel may prove equally dominant once the boat is moving ahead at her best speed.

Practical Exercises

Most boats have different handling charac-teristics in different wind strengths. Learning about them is likely to take time and the experience of varying conditions, but there are a number of basics which you can find out quickly. For example, which sail combinations are most effective?

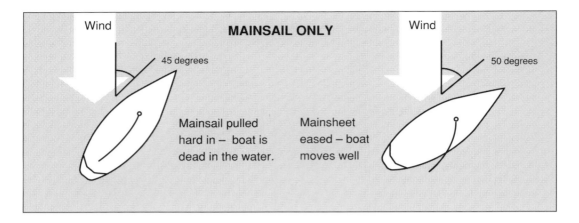

MAINSAIL ONLY

Wind

45 degrees

Mainsail pulled hard in – boat is dead in the water.

Wind

50 degrees

Mainsheet eased – boat moves well

Mainsail only

You might choose to begin with just a mainsail set. Some modern masthead-rig boats are reluctant performers under main alone. If this is the case with your yacht, the secret of coaxing her to windward will be not to try too hard. The most common mistake when working to windward without a headsail is to oversheet the main, because the boat simply dies and loses steerage way. Ease the sheet well and do not point too high. She should then come to life.

Headsail only

Sailing under a headsail alone can be more encouraging. Most modern boats will perform adequately on all points of sailing without the main. This rather gives the lie to the CE/CLR balance theory which we have described, particularly as in a firm breeze many modern yachts sail fast and are quite well balanced under headsail alone. Once they are moving through the water and heeling, they can make up to weather carrying little or no lee helm. As with sailing to windward under main alone, it is a mistake to try too hard. The boat will be relatively slow to work up momentum, and if you sheet the sail in hard she will simply

sag off to leeward and go nowhere. Start with the sheet well eased, have patience and allow the speed to build up; then you can sheet her harder and point higher as she accelerates.

Note that nearly every boat will reach

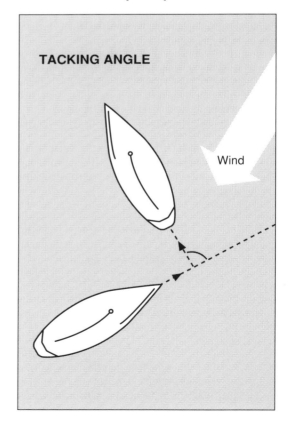

TACKING ANGLE

Wind

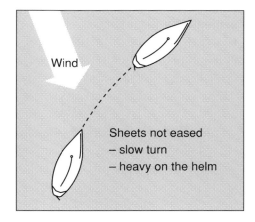

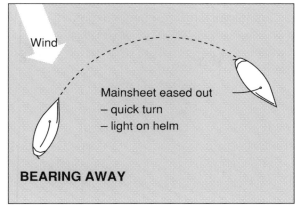

and run quite happily under main or headsail alone.

Full sail to windward

In order to determine how your boat handles under full sail, there are a number of characteristics which you need to be totally familiar with.

- *What is the boat's tacking angle?* Try going about a few times, estimating before each tack where she will be pointing as she comes out of it. The number of degrees does not really matter; the important thing is that you can judge by eye where to tack so as to clear a moored boat to windward of you. There may not be a great deal you can do to improve the pointing ability of a boat, but it is vital that you know exactly how far to stand on in order to weather an obstruction on the next tack.

- *What is the turning circle like when bearing away from close hauled?* Attempt this manoeuvre initially without touching the sheets. Just pull the tiller hard to windward. Most craft will not respond well to this treatment. They start to bear away, then they heel and develop intense weather helm to the extent that the rate of turn slows or even

stops. The boat then keeps going in a straight line with the helm feeling like a ton of bricks and the rudder stalled. She is thrown out of balance by too much sail abaft her pivot point, and by a more mysterious but equally vicious anomaly caused by her heeled hull form. After you have experienced this unpleasantness, carry out the same manoeuvre easing the sheets rapidly as you pull the helm to windward – even just the mainsheet. The result should be much more encouraging, with the boat coming upright then turning onto a downwind heading within no more than two lengths.

- *How does the yacht cope with being over-canvassed, particularly closehauled?* Narrow-beamed yachts are typically docile on the helm when over-pressed. They heel to large angles, start to lose speed and suffer an increase in leeway, but they remain easy enough to steer. On the other hand, wide-beamed boats, particularly those which carry their beam well aft, become very hard mouthed and difficult to control if asked to carry too much sail. They may even develop so much weather helm that it is almost impossible to stop them from tacking in a strong gust unless the mainsheet is eased.

- *What are the effects of being under-canvassed?* Looking at the other extreme of windward sailing characteristics, some boats don't seem to mind being 'short of rag'. They continue to handle sweetly even under so little sail that they are only making a third of their potential speed to windward. Others cannot cope with being under-sailed. As soon as the speed starts to drop in a falling wind the helm loses any feel, and directional control becomes very approximate. The situation is often aggravated by a left-over sea with waves much larger than the wind alone could raise. Certain boats can cope with this; others must be driven if they are to be kept under proper control.

Downwind

Here, characteristics vary just as much from one boat type to another as they do closehauled. Narrow boats, heavy boats and boats with long keels tend to track well and are generally easy to sail fast in a straight line, but the price is often a propensity for heavy rolling. While this may be uncomfortable it will only make the boat difficult to control in extreme cases. Wide boats, light boats and boats with short keels often feel much steadier when sailed fast downwind, yet if over-driven they will broach, rounding up to windward and being knocked almost flat. Aboard such a boat it is vital to develop an awareness of the point at which broaching becomes a possibility. Offshore a broach can be disastrous, while at close quarters it may lead to expensive entanglements with other craft.

Sternboarding

Unless she is yawl rigged, it is not always easy to sail a boat backwards. Nonetheless, it is a useful technique to acquire. Drop the jib during a practice session, bring the boat to a dead stop head to wind, then having

Sternboarding: Come head to wind, lose all way, push the boom out and steer as you would if motoring astern.

first overhauled the mainsheet, or mizzen if you have one, shove the boom out as near to athwartships as you can. (For those unfamiliar with the term, overhauling means pulling all the the mainsheet out through the blocks.) The yacht will now begin to move astern. Steer as you would under power, with the rudder itself pointing in the way you wish to move the stern. Initially, the vessel will show a strong inclination to sheer across the wind, but if you can catch her with the helm she will build up enough speed for the rudder to overcome this and away you go. You can now experiment to discover how far off dead downwind she is prepared to sail without losing control. Some boats, notably those with short keels and spade rudders, perform this feat readily, but it is not unknown for gaff cutters of 35 tons displacement to reverse when circumstances demand.

Sternboarding is of great use when anchoring and can be a help when leaving a mooring – so it is worth taking trouble over.

2 Wind and Tidal Streams

The plan for most set-piece boat handling manoeuvres is determined by the direction and strength of the wind and tidal stream. Hence the ability to assess these factors in a small local area is essential. You cannot guarantee that the tidal stream will be flowing up an estuary simply because it is flooding: there may be an eddy running the other way at the point where you plan to pick up a mooring buoy. Similarly, the fact that the wind is a westerly Force 5 in the open sea does not necessarily mean that this is what you will find at the marina berth in the lee of a block of flats. You must use your eyes and all the available clues to avoid being caught out. Never assume anything. If your plans are based on assumptions which seemed reasonable but prove flawed, they are unlikely to proceed to a trouble-free conclusion.

Note how the boats inshore are lying in completely the opposite direction to 'P16' in the foreground.

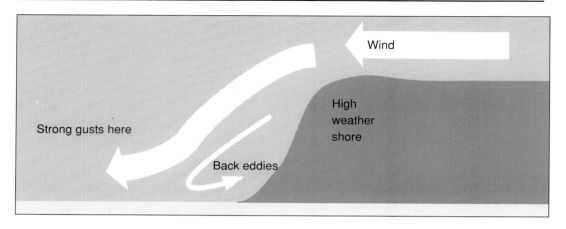

WIND AWARENESS

There is no such thing as an absolutely steady wind. Even in the ocean tradewind belts there are local variations in strength and direction. Close to land these variations are often substantial, and you need to be able to spot them. An awareness and anticipation of windshifts is frequently ascribed to local knowledge, but by keeping in mind some general rules and maintaining a sharp weather eye it is possible to predict major changes in unfamiliar places.

Obvious flat spots in the wind are found close under the lee of trees and buildings. These are local effects which cannot be extrapolated onto a larger scale. For instance on the leeward side of high land there will frequently be a band of strong wind. People talk of the wind 'falling off the top of an island'. This is a somewhat unscientific explanation of the phenomenon, but the effect undoubtedly exists as anyone who has cruised Norway will confirm. 'Funnels' between land masses tend to cause increases in wind strength, and to modify the direction of the wind so that it blows directly along the line of the funnel. The Straits of Dover, the West Solent and the Sound of Mull are typical examples.

Another local change is the readiness of the wind to bend and locally increase in strength around high headlands, such as occurs notoriously in the vicinity of Cape Finisterre.

Wind ripples

While topography can give useful clues as to likely local changes, these are best spotted by keeping an eye on natural wind indicators. Smoke from chimneys and the ensigns of moored yachts are give-aways for anybody alert enough to spot them, but the most important wind indicator of all is the appearance of the sea's surface. The breeze sets up tiny ripples on the sea's face whether it is blowing Force 1 or Force 9. These ripples, which are not to be confused with waves, run at exactly right angles to the true wind. Observe them and you have the wind direction. You can even sight across them with a compass if you require a bearing.

Never use your masthead indicator to judge wind direction for tactical purposes. All it will tell you about is the 'apparent wind', which is the true wind as modified by the boat's progress through the airstream. Apparent wind can be bent by up to 45 degrees from the real airflow in which you are manoeuvring, so while its

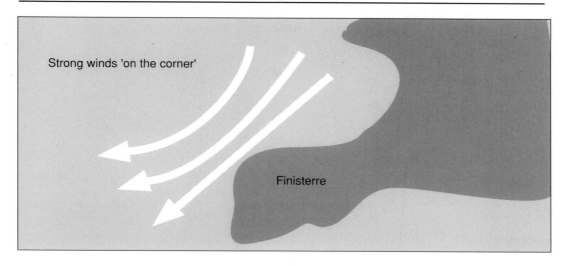

Strong winds 'on the corner'

Finisterre

direction is useful for deciding about sail changes and such like, its angle is often of little relevance to the sailor trying to work out whether or not he can lay his chosen anchoring place without putting in a tack.

Wind to beware of

Gradual variations in wind strength and direction take place with meteorological conditions, but there are two types of sudden and sometimes dramatic windshift to be wary of:

The Line Squall. Whenever an active weather front moves through it may bring strong gusts, known as line squalls. These seldom arrive unannounced, occurring as they do under a line of thick cloud. If their strength is to be of significance, the increase in white horses which they whip up will be clearly visible to windward. A doubling of the wind strength is the general order of magnitude to be expected in one of these squalls, and it may well last anything between ten minutes and half an hour before gradually dropping.

Thunderstorms. Even more dramatic wind changes may be experienced around thunderstorms. Shifts in direction of

anything up to 180 degrees, coupled with an increase in velocity from 5 to 40 knots are not uncommon. Thunderstorms seldom arrive without warning. The lightning and thunder give obvious warning of their approach, and the towering cumulus clouds which they throw up are difficult to miss. The direction of travel of a thunderstorm can however be totally unpredictable, and it is a great mistake to assume that because you are upwind of a storm you are safe from it.

A thunderhead like this is an unmistakable sign to watch out for squalls.

TIDE AWARENESS

Tide tables, tidal diamonds on charts, and tidal stream atlases can never tell the whole story of stream directions and rates. Local eddies and races occur in almost every harbour and estuary. While the locals know exactly when and where these occur, the stranger who is prepared to search for the indications can usually find most of them. The most obvious evidence is boats lying in unexpected directions on their moorings. Also observe:

- At closer range the wash around a buoy or beacon can be a useful pointer.
- Alongside a pontoon or jetty the movement of flotsam can confirm that the tidal stream is flowing as expected, or that there is a local eddy.

- A line between different textures or colours of the water is a good indication of the boundary between the main stream and an eddy, although the presence of this sort of line is by no means always significant. It may simply show the position of a sewer outfall or river water entering a harbour or estuary.
- When manoeuvring in a river around the time of the turn of the tide, you can often spot the stream by placing the boat at right angles to the river bank, lining up two objects, observing how they move against one another (a natural transit), and deducing which way you are drifting.

Water running past a buoy is the surest indication of tidal stream strength and direction.

3 Rope and Line Sense

One of the less pleasant sights and sounds of any yacht harbour is a skipper who has just loused up an apparently simple manoeuvre loudly blaming his crew for his mistake. Foul-ups undoubtedly do occur because the folks in the cockpit allowed a sheet to snarl around a winch, someone by the mast failed to haul on a halyard when a sail needed to be set quickly, or the man on the foredeck let go the anchor too soon, but there is an old adage that there is no such thing as a bad crew. There are badly trained, badly briefed and badly motivated crews. But the fact that they are badly trained, briefed or motivated is not their fault; they have simply been unlucky enough to sail with a bad skipper.

Many boat handling manoeuvres go wrong because crews, under their skipper's direction, make mistakes. It is worth looking at methods, techniques and gear which can eliminate unnecessary errors.

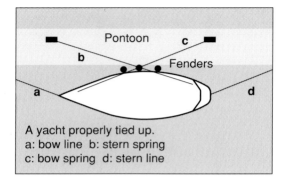

A yacht properly tied up.
a: bow line b: stern spring
c: bow spring d: stern line

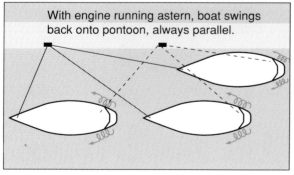

Bow line only –
boat lies bows-in

MOORING LINES

There are generally four lines used for berthing. These are the bow line, the stern line, the bow spring and the stern spring. For as simple a system to function properly, each rope must be a single unit and each must have its own cleat aboard. Tying up with four ropes is actually quicker than any other way, because there is no discussion about what is to be done and no ropes are doubled back. If a slip-rope is deemed necessary, this can be organised on departure.

An analysis of a well tied-up yacht shows that her lines work in pairs to keep her parallel to the wall or pontoon on which she is lying. Imagine a yacht tied up to a pontoon at slack water, with a very strong wind blowing along it from the direction of her bows. If she is attached to the dock by only a bow line, what will happen? She will,

of course, stay put, but her bow will be pulled in while her stern swings untidily away from the dock. Now imagine the same yacht in the same position, secured by nothing but a stern spring rigged from the extreme quarter. Her stern will tuck in to the wall, and the bow will swing away until the boat blows right round.

In the conditions described, neither line will produce a neat result on its own. But if the two are employed together and adjusted until they are the same length and at a similar angle, the boat's head will be held off by the stern spring and checked by the bow line from swinging too far. Both will be stopping her from sliding away astern, and she will lie sweetly alongside. Should the wind now switch to the boat's beam, she would blow away from the pontoon with both lines staying more or less tight. If, without adjusting either line, her engine

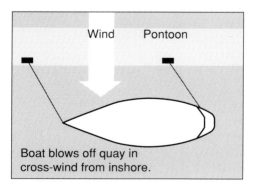

Boat blows off quay in cross-wind from inshore.

With engine running astern, boat swings back onto pontoon, always parallel.

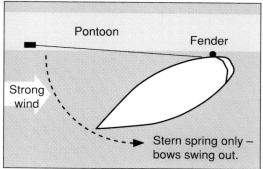

Stern spring only —
bows swing out.

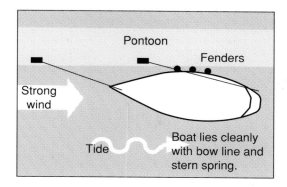

Boat lies cleanly
with bow line and
stern spring.

was run astern, the lines would act like the legs of a set of parallel rulers so that the yacht would swing back tidily alongside the woodwork, and stay there until the power was taken off.

Just as a properly rigged bow line and stern spring form a perfect pair, so do their opposite numbers, the bow spring and stern line. In order to settle the yacht with her engine going astern against stern spring and bow line, it is necessary to rig a stern line and a bow spring. The power can now be turned off, so that when the yacht tries to surge ahead she will be checked in perfect parallel by the new pair of lines. The bow spring will try to kick the stern out, but it will fail because at the same moment the stern line will be coming tight.

A further benefit of the 'one rope, one job, and springs led to the ends' rule is that if you are struggling to shove the yacht's

head or stern off the dock, your springs are already suitably placed. We've seen what happens if a boat is blown or motors astern onto a stern spring. If no other lines are present, the bow comes out as sure as tripe is served with vinegar. When you need to shove your stern off the wall, you are even better placed. Not forgetting fenders, motor ahead against a single bow spring, steer in towards the dock so that your prop wash hits the angled rudder to help the spring line, and you'll walk out of the berth with dramatic effect.

In boats with midships cleats it is possible to rig the springs the other way round, leading forward and aft from the centre of the boat, but a line thus led will not do its job properly. There are occasions when rigging the springs like this is the easiest way to hold the boat in her berth, and because of its position near the boat's

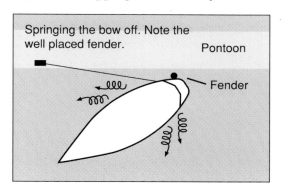

Springing the bow off. Note the well placed fender.

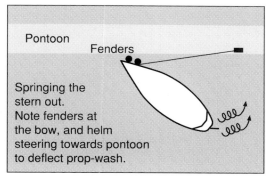

Springing the stern out. Note fenders at the bow, and helm steering towards pontoon to deflect prop-wash.

Springing the stern out by motoring ahead against the head spring.

CLR a midships spring can be useful for stopping the boat. But if springs are to be used for leaving, they are better rigged aft from the bow and forward from the stern.

Making fast

When entering or leaving a berth, there are two necessities for mooring lines - they must be secured to a cleat, bollard or ring with speed and certainty, and it is essential that they can be slipped from any of these securing devices with similar crispness, whether they are under load or not. This means that at least one end must be secured in such a way that it can be eased progressively and then let go under tension, and that each rope must do one job

only. If you are tempted to use a line for more than one job, sooner or later you will end up with a nonsense. You may get away with that practice for years in snug marinas, but try it on a serious wall with a good rise and fall of tide and you'll wish you hadn't. The line which it is necessary to adjust will always turn out to be locked up with another that cannot be moved.

Some skippers like to have lines made up with eyes spliced into the ends so they may be dropped easily over a cleat or bollard. Unfortunately such eyes never seem to be the right size for a particular job, and the splice will catch nearly every time if the line is rigged to slip when leaving the dock. Furthermore, it often cannot be passed through a small fairlead. Generally speaking, lines with plain ends

Take half a turn, two figures-of-eight, a couple of round turns and a locking hitch if you wish.

are much less likely to cause problems.

The question of how lines are secured to cleats is often a vexed one. A favourite textbook method is to take half a turn round the base, then two or three figures-of-eight, followed by a couple of round turns. There is actually nothing wrong with dispensing with the final round turns, and replacing them with a locking hitch. Traditionally, locking hitches were frowned on because natural fibre ropes shrink when wet and can rack up a locking hitch so tight that it is impossible to undo. With modern synthetic

fibres this is never a problem, but these ropes do tend to be slippery - if a locking hitch is not used to finish off the securing process, a shiny line can creep around the cleat and work loose over a period of time.

The aim of the 'textbook' method of securing to a cleat is to have a system which holds fast when you want it to, but which can be released under any amount of load. The first round turn is there so that the line can be surged (eased) round the cleat under load without risk of a sudden jerk. There is sometimes a temptation to

Remember to 'dip the eye' to allow any line to be slipped on its own.

A round turn and two half hitches.

take in a little slack on a line, by bringing a loop of the part between the boat and the dock (known as the *bight*) back round the cleat. Avoid this practice like the plague, as it makes the line totally impossible to slip under load.

If you are securing to a cleat on the dock, there is no reason why you should not·slip a bowline over the cleat for quickness, *so long as the other end of the rope is secured on board in such a way that it can be eased under load*. That way, the bowline will never be a problem. If you fail to observe this rule, one day you will end up searching for the bread-knife. When securing to a large bollard, a bowline is your only option unless the line has an enormous eye spliced into it. If the bollard

is shared by a number of other lines, the polite way to add yours is to 'Dip the eye'. This allows any line to be slipped independently.

The most suitable knot for securing a line to a ring is a round turn and two half hitches. As soon as the first turn has been taken the line can be held against a strong pull, and when the time comes to slip it is easy to undo and can be surged under control when there is a heavy load. Sometimes, you will find that a ring is sited so that groping to untie the half hitches is fiddly; for example, after dark on a crowded ring or on a mooring pile. In such a case use a long bowline instead, but always have a round turn on the ring to minimise chafe.

A round turn and two half hitches can be eased progressively under modest loading.

Stepping ashore

Every berthing manoeuvre involves either taking or passing mooring lines to the shore or to another boat. The exercise will be much simplified by estimating in advance how long each line will have to be, then making it off to approximately the right length, plus half as much again for contingencies. This is the length you should carry ashore, rather than struggle with the whole rope. Taking the lot onto the pontoon, or worse still throwing it at someone in another boat, always complicates the issue. You should finish up with any spare ends of rope on your own deck, not on someone else's or on the quayside - so you may as well start off with any extra line on board rather than ashore.

When stepping ashore take just enough rope with a margin for safety. Stand outside the guardrails, holding onto the shrouds - not up in the bows. Step ashore when it is safe - do not jump.

This is both unseamanlike and impolite: sort out the line before you pass it ashore!

Slip Ropes

There are a number of manoeuvres which require lines to be rigged as slip ropes, with the bight taken around the securing point ashore and both ends led back on board. The object of the exercise is to be able to ease the line under load and then slip it. If there is an eye or a bulky backsplice in the end of the line it may well jam at the crucial moment. The ends of mooring lines should be kept tidy with whippings, or by heat sealing if you are feeling bone idle, never with splices.

Springing the bows off the dock using a slip rope.

Fenders

People argue about the right way to secure fenders. Some like them secured to the guardrail. Others insist that the lanyard of a trapped fender can place a damagingly strong load on the wire, and that they should therefore be secured to the handrail on top of the coachroof. Against this is the view that the lanyards then become a row of trip lines along the side deck, all of which is eminently reasonable. 'Different ships, different long splices' is the only answer. There really is no absolutely right answer, and hence no 'totally wrong' securing point. Do what seems best under the circumstances and avoid the trap of being dogmatic.

The important thing is that fenders are placed at the right height. For most pontoon berths this means suspending them as low as possible without actually putting the bottom in the water. For berthing alongside another boat or a wall they must be positioned with the tops at deck level, or just under the rubbing strake if your boat

Fenders must always be at the correct height or they will ride up.

has one. On a boat with a protruding metal toe rail, you must be particularly careful about fendering when berthing amongst other boats.

There is no 'correct way' to secure fenders. The crew here is quite reasonably clove-hitching them to the top of the guardrail .

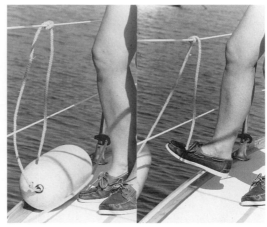

Once secured the fenders can be brought back onto the deck, ready to be kicked over the side on the final approach.

This is good winching. Three full turns...   *...and the weight directly over the winch.*

SHEETS & HALYARDS

With any modern boat, handling sheets and halyards means using winches. Considering the power they deliver, winches cause surprisingly little trouble. The first most popular mistake is having too few turns round the winch, so that when the load comes on the rope starts to slip and the crew cannot hold it. The result is either a shambles as the line escapes, or crushed fingers as the crew's hand is dragged into the winch. Even when the winch man is sensible enough to let go, he may suffer a rope burn. A winch is never secure unless

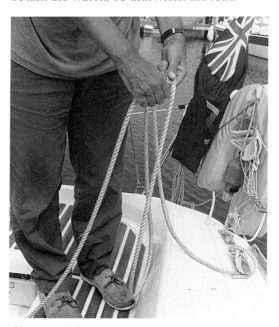

Always coil from the cleat, and always coil clockwise.

Use the palm of your hand to help ease turns under high load.

A riding turn is always the result of carelessness or a poor lead.

there are three turns around it. Should the winch be large enough, four turns are better.

The second most popular mistake is to ease a rope round a winch carelessly, and specifically from too low an angle. This causes riding turns which can be difficult to clear. The safest method is to place the flat of your hand on the turns, and help them round the barrel until the worst of the tension has been released. The only way to clear a riding turn, if you cannot take the fall

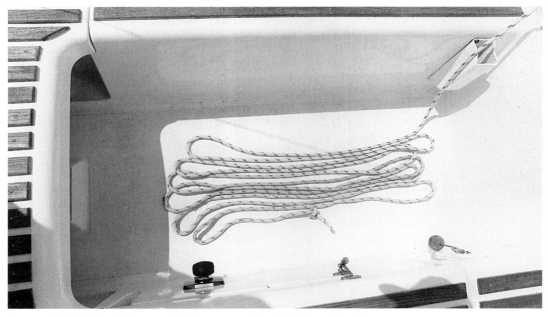

A rope flaked (faked) down will always run without kinks and snarls.

to a free winch and literally grind it out, is to
relieve the load. This is ideally done by
bending a spare line to the clew of the sail
and winding it up on a spare winch until the
offending sheet comes slack. You can then
work at the riding turn until it is cleared.
Occasionally, you will find yourself unable
to reach the clew, in which case you must
clap (another term for bend or attach) the
spare line onto the bight of the sheet using
a rolling hitch.

*Never start to coil a rope from the unsecured
(bitter) end.*

A boat with all halyards, sail controls
and reefing lines led aft may have as many
as 18 ropes terminating in the cockpit.
Leave them in a heap and you have a
recipe for snarl-ups which inevitably seem
to happen at the most inconvenient or
dangerous moments. Organisation is
essential if this snakes' wedding is to be
kept under control. Bags or shock cord are
useful for stowing the ends of halyards,
while for keeping the tails of sheets neatly
coiled and separate from each other,
determination is still the favourite tool.

A common mistake when coiling any
rope is to work from the bitter end towards
the point at which it is secured. This piles
up kinks in the rope which will jam as soon
as they reach a block or fairlead. Always
begin at the cleat, so that any twists can
drop out of the bitter end, and always coil
clockwise. The three-strand ropes in
common use are built so that a counter-
clockwise turn runs 'against the lay',
causing a single kink. Coil the whole rope
contrary to its natural tendency and you lay
up grief in multiple proportions. Some of
today's braidlines can be coiled in either
direction, but the principle should still hold.
A sailor should not have the ability to coil
'against the sun'.

Some manoeuvres depend totally for
their success on a sail being lowered
quickly. In these situations it is worth flaking
down the halyard tail to make sure that it
runs free. To achieve this, work the rope
through your hands, starting with the bitter
end, allowing its whole length to fall
naturally onto the deck in what may appear
an unruly heap. By doing this, you will have
ensured that when the halyard is let go, it is
always running from the top of the pile,
reducing the chance of a jam to the
absolute minimum.

TEAMWORK

Every manoeuvre relies to some extent upon teamwork. In some cases it is the crucial factor. It is vital therefore that the skipper explains to the crew exactly what he intends to do, what could go wrong, and what his opt-out plan might be. He should also encourage input from them, because occasionally the crew will realise that their skipper is about to attempt the impossible. By pointing out the error of his ways they may save him from embarrassment, or even a damaging fracas.

In one of the busiest south coast yacht harbours the harbourmaster keeps a small launch on patrol in the entrance on summer weekends. Traffic is heavy, so the launch can only escort a small percentage of visitors to their berths. The harbour-master's instructions on how to select boats which might benefit from a little assistance are uncomplicated. They listen to the arrivals. If the team are managing things quietly, the harbour staff tell them which berth to go to and wish them a pleasant visit. If the skipper is shouting at the crew, they accompany the yacht, assist with her lines, and ensure that her crew does as little damage as possible.

Coming alongside. Everyone ready in their places, and no shouting.

4 Mooring Manoeuvres Under Power

In many busy and crowded harbours there is now insufficient space to sail, and some authorities publish local rules to forbid the practice under any circumstances, leaving yachtsmen no option but to motor to and from their berths. Taken at face value, these two propositions might create the impression that boats are easier to handle under power than sail, but while there are certainly some situations in which sailing is not a viable option, this does not mean that handling under power requires any less skill.

In all power handling, striking the right balance between unnecessary force and faint-heartedness can be crucial. There are times when full power is needed on the engine and nothing less will do, but once you have committed yourself you have nothing left in reserve, so before you move the throttle hard against the stops be sure that there is really no alternative.

It is important to distinguish between power and speed. You should never be afraid to use plenty of power, as opposed to speed, when you need it. The precursor to a collision is usually too much power applied for too long. This can result in an excess of momentum, and it is momentum which generates the energy to create damage. The larger the boat, the slower she should enter her berth, because weight in motion equals momentum. You may be physically able to fend off a light displacement twenty footer (7m), but if a 40ft (14m) ocean cruiser with all her tanks full needs to be stopped in a hurry, it will be a more serious business.

LEAVING AN ALONGSIDE BERTH

Before you start any manoeuvre under power, it is always a good idea to check that you have drive available ahead and astern. Slip the engine into gear in each direction and make sure that you have the expected response. As with most manoeuvres, leaving an alongside berth can be childishly simple or fiendishly difficult. It all depends on the sea room and the strength and direction of the wind and tidal stream. One of the keys to good boat handling is the ability to recognise simple situations, and not to complicate them.

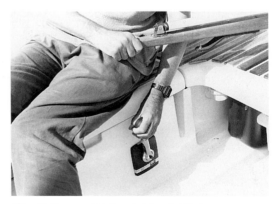

Check the engine is working before you commit yourself to a plan of action.

Offshore winds

The simplest situation for leaving an alongside berth is a light offshore wind, a gentle stream from ahead, and no boats berthed ahead or astern. All you have to do is start the engine, take your lines off the dock, step on board and motor away. It really could not be easier, so don't make it complicated by rigging a spring as a slip rope and motoring against it to slew the boat out of her berth. The wind will blow her off, very slowly, and the stream will ensure that you have steerage way almost immediately.

A strong offshore wind with a slack or feeble tidal stream is also a straightforward situation, but there is now some scope for getting it wrong so a little more control is needed. The danger is that if you try to undo the lines and step on board with them, one end of the boat will leave the berth before you are ready, with the result that your crew is left ashore. You won't be needing the springs, so you can take them off first. Now rig the head and stern lines as slip ropes. Ease them both at the same time to make sure that neither are jamming, then slip them and motor away.

A tidal stream of almost any strength from ahead would have little effect on either of these two manoeuvres. If there were an obstruction or another boat berthed close astern of you, it would be necessary to give a touch ahead on the engine to make sure that you were not carried into her. Tidal stream from astern, on the other hand, is always a nuisance. If you have two knots of stream under you as you leave a berth, you are effectively going astern through the water at two knots before you start. You must therefore accelerate through more than this speed before you have steerage-way ahead, if this is the direction in which you choose to leave.

With a strong wind off the berth, a strong stream from astern and another boat moored ahead (diagram opposite) the departure plan needs definite modification from the slack water situation. Rig the stern line and bow spring as slip ropes, taking off the stern spring and bow line in that order. Assuming you are lying starboard side to the berth, push the tiller to starboard (wheel to port) and ease the stern line so that the stern swings clear. When she has swung out to an angle of 20 degrees or so, put the engine astern and slip the stern line. As soon as the bow spring goes slack, slip it and motor out astern. You may have to reverse the helm at this stage to prevent the boat from slewing round broadside to the stream, and you should also consider

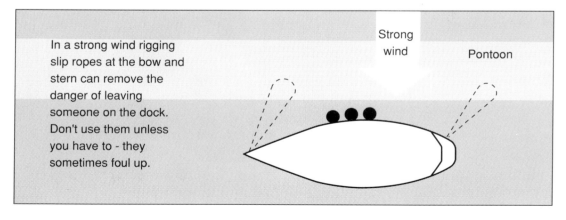

In a strong wind rigging slip ropes at the bow and stern can remove the danger of leaving someone on the dock. Don't use them unless you have to - they sometimes foul up.

Strong wind

Pontoon

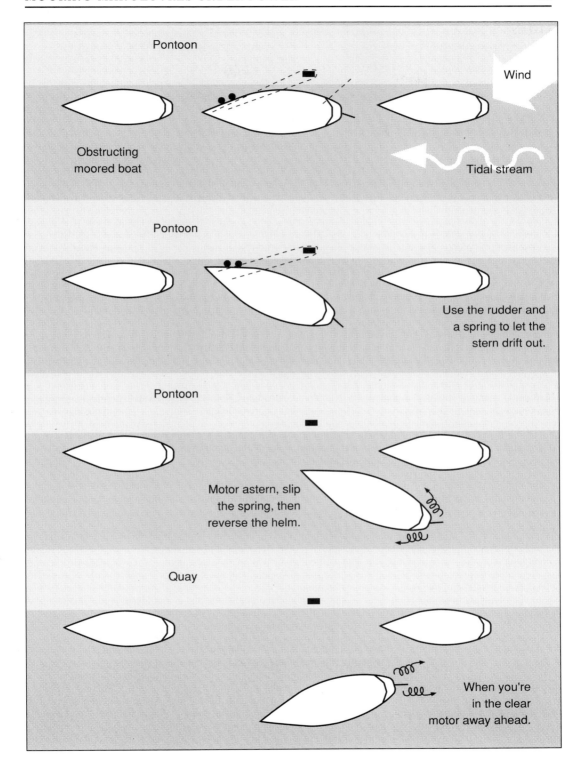

Pontoon

Wind

Obstructing
moored boat

Tidal stream

Pontoon

Use the rudder and
a spring to let the
stern drift out.

Pontoon

Motor astern, slip
the spring, then
reverse the helm.

Quay

When you're
in the clear
motor away ahead.

the effect that the yacht's tendency to prop-walk will have on the situation. Once well clear of the berth, put the engine ahead and motor away.

With no obstructions ahead of you, the same situation might be handled by using head and stern lines as slip ropes and dispensing with springs. The head rope is let go first, allowing the stern to slew into the berth and the bow to swing out a short distance as a result. The stern rope is slipped as the engine is gunned ahead. This could well accomplish the aim, so why go for the stern-first departure? For two reasons. By leaving stern first the boat was under total control at all times and there was no need to use more than minimal engine power. With the ahead departure there was a period between slipping the stern line and gathering way ahead when the boat was not under control. Success would depend on using a high level of engine power. It is always disconcerting to be in charge of a boat which will not answer her helm, and as we have discussed reliance on high levels of power is best avoided if there is an alternative available. If, for any reason, the engine does not develop the power you need, you are in trouble. Furthermore, as soon as you have put the power on, you have created a situation in which stopping will be more difficult if you are suddenly confronted with the unexpected.

Onshore winds

Leaving a berth with the wind pressing onto it requires more thought and preparation than when the yacht is being blown off. In order to lift the boat from the berth you will first have to slew one end or the other off the wall. This is because the engine will only drive ahead or astern, and

it will not move the boat sideways against the wind. In very strong breezes it will generally be easier in a modern yacht to slew the stern out and leave stern first, than to force the bow out and drive away ahead. There are good reasons for this. With the rudder positioned behind the propeller, it can be used against a spring line to push the stern sideways in the prop-wash, even though the boat is not moving through the water. The narrow bows of the boat help to allow the head to cant inwards onto the berth, and once the lines are let go the stern will naturally want to swing up into the wind. If you leave bow first, your ship's head will be blowing back onto the berth all the time until you have enough way on to counteract the tendency.

Before starting a springing-off manoeuvre in an onshore wind, it is vital to position the fenders where they are going to be needed, which will be along the inboard bow if you are swinging the stern out. One fender spare and ready for immediate use is also a good idea. Have a look at the shape of the bow in relation to the height of the pontoon to make sure that you are not going to damage anything - watch out for fresh water taps, large cleats and electricity points, and remember that a flared bow can overhang the pontoon by a surprisingly long way.

With fenders organised, take off all the lines except the bow spring and rig it as a slip rope. Motor ahead, gently at first as the spring line takes up, while steering so as to push the bow in towards the berth, then use no more power than you need to slew the boat through about 40 degrees. Now go firmly astern, slip the spring line and motor out of the berth. Remember that your stern will want to prop-walk. If this is in your favour, well and good. If not, allow for it and

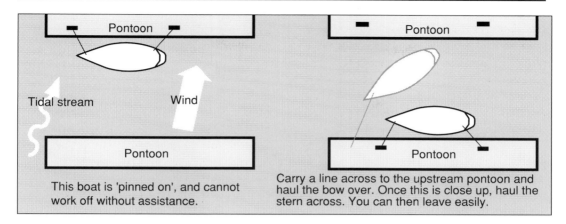

This boat is 'pinned on', and cannot work off without assistance.

Carry a line across to the upstream pontoon and haul the bow over. Once this is close up, haul the stern across. You can then leave easily.

spring further out than you might otherwise have done.

The theory is simple, but the judgement of how far to spring the boat is more difficult. This is a 'forcing manoeuvre', because for most of it you are driving the boat against the direction in which she would prefer to move. A degree of commitment is needed, and hesitancy at the point of putting the engine astern can be fatal, since a failure to apply plenty of astern power will see the boat blown back onto the berth. As we have noted, the stern's natural tendency to seek the wind will help to lift the boat out of the berth, but the same forces will be blowing the bows to leeward. If you have not sprung the boat far enough or are insufficiently firm with the astern power after slipping, you risk scraping the bow along the berth or being carried onto a boat tied up astern. Also remember that before the yacht has gathered stern-way, her inclination to spin her stern into the wind and her propeller paddle-wheel effect will be much stronger than anything the rudder can do.

With tidal stream from ahead the best way out of the berth will be to spring the bow off using the stern spring. In some ways this is an easier manoeuvre since the stream helps to lift the boat out of her berth, but it is another one in which hesitation can be fatal. As soon as you have the bow well off the berth, go for plenty of power ahead. In any of these forcing manoeuvres in which you have to drive the boat against the wind a foul-up on the spring line is fatal. Make sure that both ends can be released and if the line catches on the cleat or ring ashore let go both ends. You can always come back and pick it up, but once committed to the manoeuvre you cannot change your mind halfway through.

With both wind and stream setting onto a pontoon berth you may be able to spring off, but you will have to slew the boat through close to 90 degrees. If wind or stream are unusually strong this may prove impossible, or put so much weight on the boat as to be inadvisable. In a marina berth you may manage to overcome the problem by taking lines to an upwind berth and hauling the boat across to it, transforming an almost impossible situation into a very easy one. Warping a boat from one berth to another often looks as if it will require large amounts of strength on the lines. So it will, if you try to move the whole boat in one go, but the muscle required is very much less if you shift one end at a time.

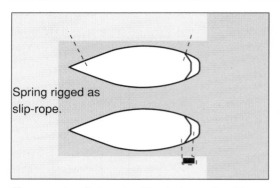
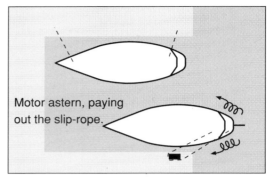

Use an extended spring line to turn a boat in a cramped space in a marina, ready to motor out from the end of the pontoon.

The extended spring line

Leaving a pontoon in a marina where the berths are closely packed, an extended spring line can be a useful means of turning the boat after she has left the berth. Motor astern out of the berth with a long spring rigged as a slip rope from your inboard quarter to the outer end of the berth. Let it run until the bow is clear of the berth, then take a turn; keep motoring astern and swing the boat around on the spring until she is pointing towards open water. Put the engine ahead, slip the spring and recover it quickly, taking care that it does not foul and is not allowed anywhere near the propeller.

Leaving a raft-up

One of the more complex unberthing manoeuvres is extracting yourself from the middle of a raft of moored boats, because you must consider not only how you are going to slide out, but also how the boats outside you are going to re-moor after you have left. There will usually be plenty of assistance available from the crews of the other boats, but if not you will have to leave one of your own crew ashore to re-secure the raft, collecting him afterwards from the outermost boat.

The direction in which you leave will be directed by the tidal stream. First make sure that the boats outside you are well secured to each other. Then remove their shore lines on the down-tide end, leading a long line from your outboard neighbour's down-tide end which goes up-tide of you and onto your inboard neighbour. Shuffle out of the stack, using a combination of engine and pushing, making sure that someone is taking in the slack on the long line as you go. Once you are clear of the stack this line can be used to haul the boats that were outside you back into position. Their up-tide shore lines will have to be shortened as they will all be a little closer to the quay or pontoon. Their down-tide shore lines must be replaced. It may be a help if one of the outside boats starts its engine and acts as a tug to keep the raft in place.

COMING INTO AN ALONGSIDE BERTH

Putting a boat into an alongside berth is in many ways easier than taking her out of one. You have more options available, since you can often decide which berth you want to use and which way round you want to approach it. You start the manoeuvre with the boat moving and under control. You can make a dummy run, a few boat

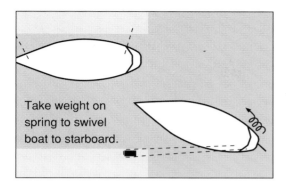

Take weight on spring to swivel boat to starboard.

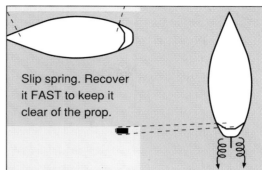

Slip spring. Recover it FAST to keep it clear of the prop.

lengths off the berth to get the measure of the rate of the stream and the strength of the wind, and if things aren't developing as you expect you can usually abort the attempt, go round and try again.

Never make the mistake of only considering how you are going to work into a berth. Ponder also upon how you are going to leave and how comfortable the stay is going to be. If you are spending the night on board it will normally be more pleasant if the wind is from ahead rather than astern, and pressing the boat off rather than onto the berth. By thus arranging matters, the breeze will not be blowing into the cockpit and down the companionway; neither will squeaky fenders ruin a good night's sleep.

The basic approach

In calm conditions with no tidal stream the basic approach to an alongside berth is made as slowly as is reasonable, bearing in mind the need to maintain steerage way, at an angle of 10 to 15 degrees to the line of the berth. If you have a right-handed propeller which kicks your stern to port under astern propulsion, you will select port side to the dock. Swing the stern in, using the helm and the paddle-wheel effect as you put the engine astern to take way off. As the fenders touch the pontoon, the crew

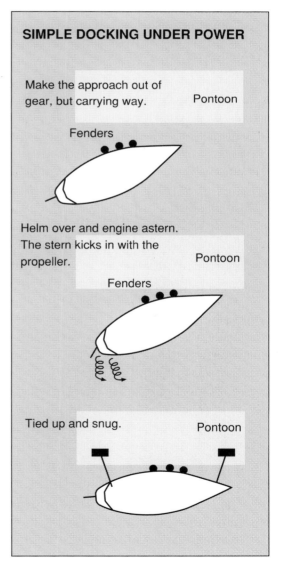

SIMPLE DOCKING UNDER POWER

Make the approach out of gear, but carrying way.   Pontoon

Fenders

Helm over and engine astern. The stern kicks in with the propeller.   Pontoon

Fenders

Tied up and snug.   Pontoon

Make a steady, slow appraoch. The crew should be ready, but only jump ashore in the final moments as the boat touches.

take the head and stern lines ashore. Exactly when to go astern and how much power to apply is a matter of judgement, and depends on the weight of the boat and the efficiency of the prop in delivering

The boat can be straightened up once you have secured it at both stern and bow.

power astern. Naturally, if your prop-walk in astern is to starboard, you should opt for starboard side to.

Concentration is needed in any berthing manoeuvre, so avoid distractions wherever possible. Rig fenders early and make up the lines to the right length. As a general rule it is easiest to take the lines ashore from a position by the shrouds. Lead them through their fairleads forward and aft, taking care not to loop them round the guardrails, and have the crew who are taking them ashore standing outside the guardrails holding onto the shrouds in the final stages of the approach. Make sure that nobody tries to step directly from inside the guardrails onto a thin finger pontoon - it will sink a little under their weight, sometimes with disastrous results. Keep the rest of the crew out of your line of sight, either sitting down or standing on the disengaged side. It may be necessary to remind overzealous hands not to jump for the dock with a cry of "Geronimo!", and to recommend them not to heave their lines to the first dockside loafer who offers his services, when they are shortly to be placed alongside the wall in a proper, seamanlike manner.

The ability to operate the throttle and gear lever almost instinctively is important, because otherwise they can be something

of a nuisance. Some skippers use their feet for this, because with the lever mounted low down in the cockpit, getting a hand to it means bending down and taking your eyes off the line of approach. On the other hand, it is difficult to get exactly the amount of power you want if you use a welly-clad foot

The crew have bow line and stern line ready on the side deck.

The whole docking procedure should be calm and unflustered. Beware of accidents when an over-enthusiastic crew jumps off and misses the dock - it happens!

to move the lever. How you choose to do it is a matter of personal choice. You can even have one of the crew deal with the controls to your instructions, but before you do so make sure that his interpretation of "Slow", "Half" and "Full ahead" is the same as yours. "A touch more astern" is a somewhat imprecise request, and may produce something excitingly different from the result you were expecting.

Sail Training skippers in charge of large yachts often hand the helm to one of the crew and give them orders, because they prefer to be able to move around the deck, enjoying the best possible sight line rather than being tied to the helm. This may well be a good idea for them, but in a smaller vessel, or one in which you are not trying to find a job for everybody, it usually makes life more difficult. In light boats the reaction to a gust of wind is very fast and the counteraction on the helm must be equally rapid, so the time delay induced by having to pass helm orders is normally unacceptable.

Docking in wind and tide

The basic 'calm wind no stream' approach requires extending to cope with wind and tide. All boats make increasing amounts of leeway as they slow down, so the general rule with the wind blowing onto the berth is to come in with the boat heading at a

shallower angle, and at a steeper angle
with the wind blowing off. In anything up to
a moderate breeze the actual direction of
travel through the water is about the same
as in the calm wind situation. To make sure
you are holding the boat on the correct line
of approach, particularly in a tideway, find
a transit between something on the berth
and an object behind it. This will give an
immediate indication if you are drifting left
or right.

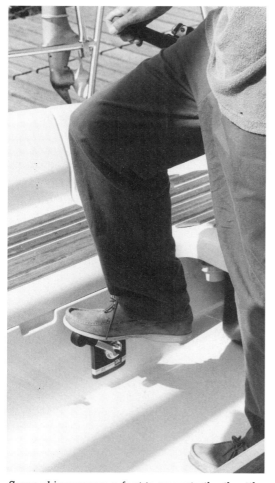

*Some skippers use a foot to operate the throttle
handle. That way their view forward is never
interrupted by having to bend down.*

Strong offshore winds

With a strong wind blowing off the berth it
is necessary to approach at a higher speed
and a steeper angle. In a light, short-keeled
boat with considerable windage it may be
impossible to lay the boat parallel to the
berth, because as you swing alongside and
slow down you will be blown off too quickly
for the crew to get ashore with the lines.
The solution to this problem is to nudge the
bow up to the berth and send the bow
spring and stern line ashore. Once these
are on, you can slack away on the bow
spring until the two lines are the same
length, by which time the boat will be
beam-on to the dock. Now motor ahead
against the two lines and she will walk
sweetly in. If there is no room ahead, use the
lines as stern spring and bow line instead,
then go astern. In either case, there will be
no need for unseemly heaving and hauling.

If you can't cope with so much
technicality, you can always rig a stern line
after the bows are secure and heave her in
using either a winch or the strength God
gave. Another way to deal with a strong
offshore wind, particularly if you are short-
handed, is to take a single line ashore from
an amidships cleat. Once this is secure you
may be able to motor ahead against it using
helm 'to taste', and spring the boat into the
berth. The spring line rigged from
amidships is particularly useful in berthing
manoeuvres. On account of its position
close to the CLR, about which the boat
pivots, it can be used as the 'emergency
brakes' because it will stop the boat without
slewing her. A line from the bow is a messy
way of stopping a boat in her berth, for it
pulls the front end hard against the pontoon
and causes the stern to kick out. A stern
rope is better, but it will jam the stern in
and throw the bow out.

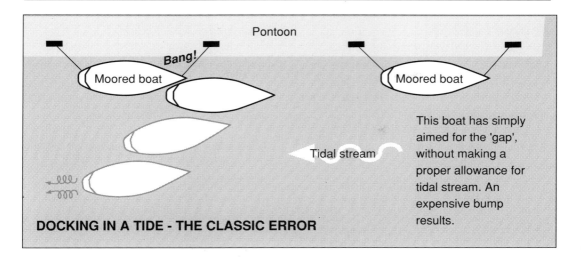

DOCKING IN A TIDE - THE CLASSIC ERROR

This boat has simply aimed for the 'gap', without making a proper allowance for tidal stream. An expensive bump results.

Strong onshore winds

Berthing in a strong onshore wind is really quite simple. The approach needs to be fairly fast to reduce leeway, with a corresponding increase in the power used astern to take way off. The most common mistake is to over compensate for the effect of the wind and stop too far off the berth, which allows speed to pick up sideways and results in a rather heavy landing. As long as the boat is well fendered this seldom does any damage but it feels horrible. As with all berthing manoeuvres, try to use prop-walk to your advantage, particularly in a situation like this where you will be pouring on astern power just as you come alongside. You are more likely to achieve a tidy result if you are not fighting the propeller.

Cross-tidal sets

Tidal stream across a berth has much the same effect as wind, and is dealt with in largely the same way. The only difference is that the stream moves the boat sideways at exactly the same speed when she is moving through the water as it does when she is stopped relative to it (though not necessarily stationary relative to the dock and the sea bed).

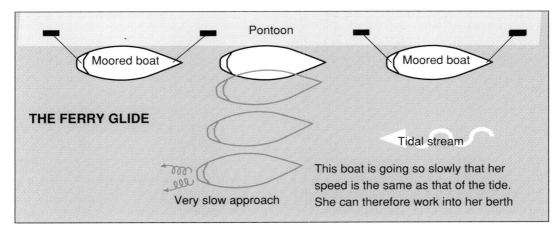

THE FERRY GLIDE

Very slow approach

This boat is going so slowly that her speed is the same as that of the tide. She can therefore work into her berth

Berthing up-tide

Tidal stream from ahead makes most berthing manoeuvres easier, because the boat is still moving ahead relative to the water and retains steerage-way even when she is stopped relative to the berth. For this reason, always berth up-tide if it is humanly possible to do so. There is one trap to be wary of - coming alongside short, and being caught in the angle between the berth and a boat astern. Once in the trap there is no escape, and the result is usually a locking of guard-rails which is always messy. The problem can be avoided by starting the approach aiming for a point slightly ahead of the berth, or ideally, 'ferry-gliding' in. This delightful technique sees the boat motoring head-up to the strong tide, parallel to and a few boats' lengths away from her berth. She is stemming the stream and stationary relative to the ground and the berth. After taking a transit on the berth, her bow is nudged in towards it just enough to allow her to slide sideways into her chosen spot. The manoeuvre is beautiful in its simplicity and effectiveness, but it all depends on a good transit.

Down-tide berthing

This would only be attempted under unusual circumstances, such as a marina berth offering no option to approach in the proper, up-tide way. Tidal stream from astern is much more awkward to handle, as the boat loses steerage way while she is still moving ahead relative to the berth. The best approach is as nearly as possible parallel to the berth, a situation in which the amidships spring, and if possible the creative use of prop-walk really come into their own. If you are berthing against the propeller, you will have no option but to take off the last of your way with the spring line, because if you use the engine the boat will prop-walk her stern out across the tide. Send your best crew ashore with the line and have them clap a loose turn onto a bollard, bringing on the tension as the rope surges, taking off the last of your way as it does so.

The worst possible combination is wind off the berth and tidal stream from astern. Start the approach aiming for a point just astern of the berth, otherwise you will finish up making the final approach at too steep an angle, securing your bows while the stern is carried out and past the berth, eventually swinging right round and hitting the boat in the berth ahead. If, in the final stages of the approach, you feel that the angle to the berth is too steep, abort and go round again.

Berthing stern-first

Occasionally it is necessary to enter a berth stern-first, which is seldom easy because most boats steer better ahead than astern. When going backwards the pivot point moves right aft, and given reasonable way this creates the impression that while one has control over the stern, the bow is wandering around at random. It is usually easier to steer facing aft, as this removes the mental gymnastics of trying to work out how to move the wheel or tiller to turn in a particular direction. In fact, steering astern when facing aft is exactly the same as looking forward when going ahead. If directional control is difficult, remember that you can always give a burst ahead on the engine against the rudder to correct an unwanted swing. Unless you are berthing down-tide, concentrate on getting the stern into the berth and secure, then warp the bow in.

General advice

Throughout this section, we have looked at only a few different combinations of wind and tidal stream in order to keep the explanations reasonably short. In practice there are of course an infinite number of possibilities, but the basic principles involved do not change. As we have said, the angle and speed of approach, together with the initial aiming point for any berthing manoeuvre are determined by wind and tidal stream components along and across the berth. Whatever the circumstances, you must decide on the strength and importance of each, then formulate a workable plan. Before committing yourself to an approach, rehearse it mentally, producing a picture of how each stage will look and feel. If the actuality begins to seem markedly different from the rehearsal in your head, you are probably about to get into trouble - so throw it away, go round, and try again.

TURNING IN A CHANNEL

Most boats can be turned round in a channel little wider than their own length. The technique for achieving this varies hardly at all whether you are steering a small yacht or a large coaster, and the skill should be mastered by practising before you try it in anger.

Calm conditions

In calm conditions the easiest direction of turn will be dictated by whether your propeller is left or right-handed. Let us assume that the stern will be kicked to starboard when going ahead, to port when going astern. The paddle-wheel effect is invariably more useful when going astern, so the choice for a right-handed propeller will be to turn to starboard. Position the

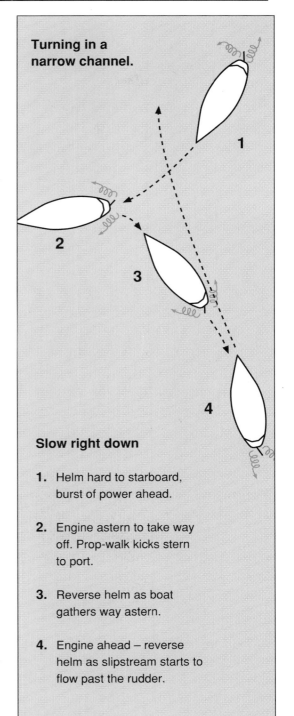

Turning in a narrow channel.

Slow right down

1. Helm hard to starboard, burst of power ahead.

2. Engine astern to take way off. Prop-walk kicks stern to port.

3. Reverse helm as boat gathers way astern.

4. Engine ahead – reverse helm as slipstream starts to flow past the rudder.

Start the turn – keep an eye on the stern.

Engine astern to take off headway.

boat halfway between the centre and port side of the channel, put the engine in neutral, and let her slow right down. Start the turn by giving a burst ahead and putting the helm hard to starboard. Depending on the displacement of your boat and the power of your engine, this burst may last from two to ten seconds, but the aim is to direct as much water as possible across the rudder without building up too much speed. When you have built up headway to the extent that you need to apply the brakes to keep her off the starboard side of the channel, put the engine astern, leaving the helm to starboard because the water is still flowing across the rudder from forward to aft. As the prop-walk kicks in, the boat will pull herself into the turn. In many boats, this force is so strong that there is no purpose to reversing the helm as the boat gathers the minimal sternway the manoeuvre requires; but if space is running out ahead, it may be politic to actually move the boat astern. In this case, the right time to reverse the helm is just as she starts to gather stern-way. Do not do so while she is moving ahead, because the rudder is still functioning in its normal mode.

As you run out of room astern, put the engine ahead. Since you will have

slipstream across the rudder almost immediately, make sure you are steering hard into the turn. Continue backing and filling like this as many times as it takes to complete the turn. With the exception of the initial burst ahead you should not need to use very much power, either ahead or astern.

Strong cross-winds

With a cross wind of any strength, paddle-wheel effect may cease to be the dominant factor, being replaced by the tendency for the stern to seek the wind and the head to 'blow off'. The short turn manoeuvre is carried out in much the same way, with alternate power ahead and astern, but the initial direction of turn should be into wind. If this coincides with helpful paddle-wheel effect the manoeuvre will generally remain feasible. If not, you may find the boat refuses. The crucial point is persuading the bows to pass through the wind. Thereafter, the rest is easy.

The anchor-assisted turn

With a headwind at the start of a turn no problems are likely. In strong following winds however, it may occasionally prove impossible to prop-walk your bow past the breeze, and as we have explained the

Prop walk kicks stern to starboard.

Reverse helm as boat gathers sternway.

Reverse helm again as the engine is put ahead.

The turn complete.

heavy crosswind can also be a killer. In such cases, the only way to turn the vessel will be to let go an anchor over the bow as you are headed downwind, snub the cable carefully, and use this to bring the boat's head to the gale. Don't be tempted to lay out a huge scope. If you do, recovering the hook will be hard work and could prejudice the success of the manoeuvre.

The anchor doesn't have to dig in fully; it must merely produce enough drag for the boat to pivot around it.

So manoeuvrable are today's yachts that such extremes are unlikely to be met in the sailing lifetime of most modern yachtsman. Those who skipper larger craft would do well to bear the technique in mind however. Coasters use it regularly, as

ANCHOR ASSISTED TURNS

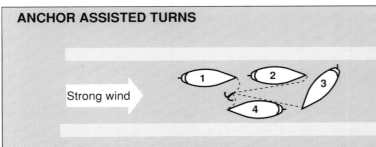

Strong wind

1. Let go anchor.
2. Let anchor cable run.
3. Snub with helm hard over - boat will spin on her anchor as the cable comes taut.
4. Recover anchor as you pass over it.

do certain schooners whose windage forward can render close-in turns a source of concern for their crews.

Tidal stream

Tidal stream does nothing to modify the speed at which a boat will turn, because the whole vessel is being carried along at the same rate. If you want to keep a boat under control at as slow a speed as possible relative to the land, your efforts will be more effective if you stem the tide. This does not however mean that a boat will turn more quickly into the tide than down-tide. She is floating in the water, not on the river bed beneath it, and if the whole mass of water is moving over the ground, the boat will be carried bodily with it while she is executing any manoeuvre at all. In other words, she will stay in the same parcel of water; but if by the time she has completed her turn this water has moved to a different geographical location, she will have been carried with it, no matter which way she may have been pointing at the start and end of the manoeuvre.

MOORING BUOYS

Coming to a buoy under power is similar to coming alongside, but it is easier in that you can approach from any direction. This allows you to head into the tidal stream, or if the stream is weak into the wind. There is a certain amount of scope in the ground tackle of all mooring buoys, so you do not have to stop dead as soon as the crew can reach the buoy. Indeed, the pickup will be easier if you reach it with a little way on.

Like most manoeuvres, approaching a mooring is simpler with a moderate tidal stream. As you stem the flow and creep up to the buoy you will have plenty of

steerage-way through the moving water, a factor which is particularly useful in a stiff wind. The main source of practical difficulty in picking up a buoy is that the helmsman usually loses sight of it before it is within reach. This problem can be at least partially solved, and the crew work simplified, if the buoy is picked up on one side just forward of the shrouds. In a cross-wind it is best to lay your weather side to the buoy, so that the boat is not blown over the mooring. In light winds it is easiest to pick up on the same side as the engine controls, so the helmsman does not have to reach across the cockpit to adjust speed or go astern.

While picking up the buoy on one side

When mooring under power the buoy is best placed on the shoulder of the yacht for the pick-up. This makes the job easier and improves the helmsman's view.

helps the helmsman, it does not totally solve the line-of-sight problem, so good communication with the foredeck is important. It can help if the crew points at the buoy, giving direction and distance to go. The second problem likely to be encountered is judging when the boat is no longer moving. It is no use looking over the side, because this will only tell you about her way through the water. What you want to know is when she has stopped relative to the ground. The only satisfactory means of achieving this is by watching a transit on the beam.

Extreme wind conditions

In winds of gale force it is occasionally more practical to pick up a buoy heading directly to leeward. It is almost impossible to hold a boat head to wind at slow speed in 50 knots of wind, but it is relatively easy to hold a downwind heading by using carefully applied power astern. The downwind approach also has the advantage that helmsman and crew are not blinded by having to peer into driving spray and rain. In addition, the motion of the boat is likely to be easier.

ANCHORING

The most difficult part of anchoring is laying the hook exactly where you want it to dig into the bottom. Your greatest desire will be to lie in a sheltered spot as convenient as possible for the landing place, with enough water to float at low tide, yet as shallow as possible so that you will not have miles of cable to recover. Tragically, everyone else wants to be there too.

Selecting your berth in a crowded anchorage is a matter of judgement. The great question is how close to other boats can you safely lie? The answer depends on whether or not their swinging characteristics are likely to be compatible with yours. If they are, they will lie to wind or

On a yacht with no windlass, flake out the required scope of cable on deck before letting go to ensure it runs free.

tide in a similar manner and you will all stay out of bother. If not, grief and woe will be your portion - usually at around 0100.

Careful preparation is essential for successful anchoring. In a small vessel this usually means having the desired scope of cable or warp flaked on deck, ready to run (three times the greatest depth of water for chain, and five times for rope are safe guidelines for scope in easy conditions). The favoured line of approach is generally on the same heading as you will lie, relative to wind or stream, after you have anchored. Look at the aspects of similar craft, and mirror them. Motor up gently, stopping over the selected spot, confirming with the echo sounder that you have the expected depth of water. Ideally, you should gather a touch of stern way before letting go. Keep motoring astern as the cable is laid out so that it cannot pile up in a heap on the sea bed. Failure to do this is a sure-fire guarantee for problems later on. Take the engine out of gear as the last of the measured length of cable runs over the roller, then watch beam transits carefully to note when the boat begins to lose way. This means the anchor is digging in. At this point, before she begins 'bouncing' ahead against the cable, engage astern gear once more and feed on a steady run of power. The boat will creep astern then bring up firmly against her cable. The transits will tell you what is happening, and an eye on the cable will ensure that it, too, is stable. Now you know you are anchored and can safely leave the yacht to her own devices. Pick a new transit after she has settled to check for dragging. Don't bother with your hand-bearing compass. A bearing is a blunt instrument compared with a transit, and only in the rarest of circumstances will one be of any practical help at all. When you are entirely satisfied, go and inspect the level in the whisky bottle.

Do not worry if you experience difficulties keeping the boat pointing towards her anchor as you lay out the cable. Usually this is not a problem, other than in the mind of the skipper. If the wind or stream are carrying her away from the pick (another term for hook or anchor) it does not matter if the yacht is lying at right angles to the lead of the cable. As soon as the cable comes taut, she will swing to her anchor and you can give that run of power to dig it in securely.

Weighing anchor

Weighing anchor under power should present few problems. The secret is good communication between foredeck and

When selecting a transit, try to pick a 'sensitive' one, with plenty of distance between the front and back marks. Here, the buoy and the block of flats are ideal.

cockpit, so that the helmsman can keep the load off the cable and make the crew's work as light as possible. Should the crew lack the strength required to break the hook out of the bottom, shorten the cable then motor full astern. Nine times out of ten this will succeed. If it fails, ease away a longer length of cable then run at it ahead, building up as much way as possible. Should this drastic measure also fail, you almost certainly have a fouled anchor. Either grope for the seamanship manual, wait for low water and take a swim, or call a diver. If the anchor is buoyed with a rope from its crown so as to enable it to be cleared from any fouling obstruction, try to recover the buoy as early as possible. Propellers seem to be magnetic to buoys and tripping lines.

A pre-rigged tripping line will generally clear a fouled anchor, but beware of wrapping it up with the propeller.

PILE MOORINGS

Berthing between two piles is a practice common only in the Solent and one or two rivers in the Thames Estuary. If you keep your boat on piles you will almost certainly have mooring lines rigged permanently to them, joined by a light line with a pick-up buoy in the middle. With this arrangement you can virtually treat your mooring as an alongside berth. As a visitor's berth between piles is unlikely to have this arrangement, you will have to put a line out

Photos left to right: A. Approach on the downwind side. Take the sternline forward to the first pile.
B. Pay out the sternline as the boat moves ahead to the second pile.
C. Attach the headrope with the pile alongside the bow, not 'over the front'.
D. All secure and middled up.

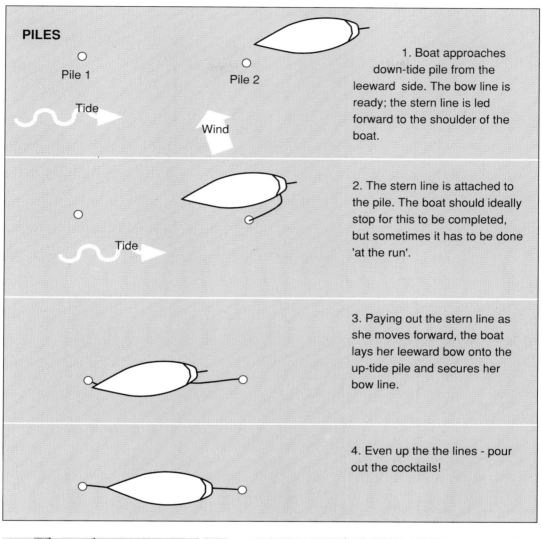

PILES

Pile 1

Pile 2

Tide

Wind

1. Boat approaches down-tide pile from the leeward side. The bow line is ready; the stern line is led forward to the shoulder of the boat.

2. The stern line is attached to the pile. The boat should ideally stop for this to be completed, but sometimes it has to be done 'at the run'.

Tide

3. Paying out the stern line as she moves forward, the boat lays her leeward bow onto the up-tide pile and secures her bow line.

4. Even up the the lines - pour out the cocktails!

C

D

The on-board view of the operation. It pays to remember that piles are frequently barnacle encrusted, and one crew should be ready to fend off if necessary while the other secures the line.

to each pile, forward and aft.

Piles are normally oriented to line up with the tidal stream, so it should always be possible to approach the berth stemming the tide. The basic method is to approach the first pile stemming the stream, and either stop with the pile on the shoulder of the boat (just forward of the shrouds) in order to attach the stern line, or secure to it on the way past. With the stern dealt with, the boat continues to the second pile where the bow line is made fast, the yacht finally dropping back so that she is middled up between the two.

Success depends very much on how smart the crew can be with the first line. This needs to be a long one because most people prefer to pass it through the mooring ring on the pile as a slip, bringing the end back on board. Before starting the approach the end should be taken through a fairlead on the quarter, and led forward to just ahead of the widest part of the boat. Passing the line through the mooring ring is easier for two people, one to lift the ring on its lanyard, the other to pass the line. If the ring proves difficult to lift, don't waste any

time with it; just pass the line round the bar on which the ring slides, or even right round the pile. It is vital that the after pile-line runs freely. If it snags the boat will stop and unless it is very calm or the helmsman very lucky, the manoeuvre will have to be aborted. If your crew are quick on their knots, they may choose to ease the possibility of a snarl-up by forgetting about the slip rope, tying the line directly to the ring with a round turn and a long bowline instead. A single-part line runs cleaner than a slip, and you have only half the chance of running out of rope. Note that when approaching the forward pile, the crew's job will be made easier if the pile can be brought close to one side of the bow rather than approached directly bow on.

Once you have mastered the technique, picking up piles in calm conditions should present no hardships. A cross-wind makes it more difficult. The approach is best made to leeward of the first pile, because with the boat moving very slowly she will be making a fair amount of leeway and hence will be angled somewhat across the piles to hold the

Leaving piles is best effected by easing the bow line until you are close enough to the stern pile to let it go in light weather, or rig it as a slip in a breeze. Once done, the yacht can move ahead and deal similarlly with the bow line. Both lines can then be slipped at leisure.

Another use for piles. A deep-keeled yacht can dry out safely, so long as she keeps a small list in towards the piles. Take steps to ensure she cannot, under any circumstances, fall outwards. This yacht has hung weights from her boom, or sometimes a halyard may be led ashore.

required track between them. This angle is impossible to achieve unless the boat passes to leeward of the first pile.

NO ENGINE! NO SAILS!

With a disabled engine and no wind, progress becomes difficult. However, a tender with a small outboard is capable of towing a relatively large yacht in a calm. If you are trying to put her into a berth, the best way is not to tow from ahead but to secure the tender alongside. This gives much better control and makes communication between the helmsman of the yacht and the helmsman of the tender much easier. Towing like this is not a viable proposition in a seaway or in any strength of wind, but if you have wind you will be able to sail.

The tender should be secured well aft, with tight bow and stern lines and springs from both ends. If it is tied too far forward, steering will be impossible and the yacht will simply be pushed round in circles. With a small engine to move a comparatively heavy boat, acceleration will be slow. Given time, speed should build up to a couple of knots. The ability of the tender's engine to stop the yacht will be severely limited, partly because outboards are

seldom very efficient when put astern, always assuming there is a reverse gear fitted. Furthermore, it will tend to push the stern sideways as much as arrest forward movement.

MEDITERRANEAN MOOR

Mediterranean mooring, berthing bow or stern-on to a wall, is seldom seen in tidal waters. It only really works in non-tidal areas such as the Med or Scandinavia. Small boats, up to about 40ft (12m), usually opt to moor with their bows to the wall because it is far simpler to drop a stern anchor and go ahead into the berth than it is to attempt to manoeuvre stern-to. Furthermore, on-board privacy is enhanced with the cockpit and companionway pointing seaward rather than towards the quay. Larger boats tend to berth stern-to because the weight of their ground tackle calls for some sort of powered windlass, which is generally only available forward.

Bow-to mooring

Make two mooring lines ready, one on each bow, and prepare an anchor aft with its cable free to run. Motor towards the berth, letting go the stern anchor about three lengths short of it, or a little further if

For a bow-to mooring approach the berth slowly. Drop the kedge anchor over the stern when still well out. Let it run until you can send your bow lines ashore, with one from each side. Secure the bow, then 'set' the stern anchor by heaving in the warp.

the water is unusually deep. Pay out the cable under control to make sure that it is laid out along the bottom. Take the way off, either by going astern or by taking the weight on the anchor. Make sure, however, that the cable is not left taut as you arrive at the berth, or the boat will be pulled astern just as the foredeck crew steps ashore with the bow lines. Secure one line off each side of the bow, then ease back a foot or two, taking up the slack in the anchor cable.

Unlike Norway or Sweden, it is rare to find an empty quay in a Mediterranean harbour. As a result, you will usually be berthing in the gap between two other boats, which means fenders on both sides. Before starting the approach, take a good look at how your neighbours-to-be are lying, noting in particular the lead of their anchor lines. You must place your anchor between theirs, not across either of them. Cross-winds obviously make the manoeuvre somewhat more challenging, but by keeping an eye on leeway with a transit to guide you into the berth, there should be no undue difficulty. Leaving the berth is simply a matter of slipping the head lines and recovering the anchor, after pulling yourself astern out of the berth. Steer sensibly as the cable is hauled in, or weighing anchor will be hard work.

Stern-to mooring

The technique of berthing stern-to is similar

Moored bow-to, the two head ropes hold the boat in position.

to that described above. The only additional problem is keeping the boat running straight as you back into the berth, though this can be minimised by taking prop-walk into account and giving due consideration to any cross-wind. If, after taking all these precautions, you start to sheer off-line, you can usually straighten her up by holding onto the cable momentarily. Don't allow the foredeck to snub the cable completely, on pain of having their grog stopped for a week. If they do, your efforts are doomed, and since the average Mediterranean port is a fine and public place, your shame will be witnessed by an informed and appreciative crowd.

5 Mooring Manoeuvres Under Sail

Since sailing a boat inside any but the most spacious harbours will represent something of a challenge to most yachtsmen, it is natural enough to ask "Why sail in harbour? Why not play safe and motor at all times?". There are two answers to this. First, sailing is fun and there is a great deal of satisfaction to be gained from it. Secondly, if you cruise for long enough, the day will come when you will have to berth without the benefit of auxiliary power. A flat battery, mechanical failure or a rope round the propeller will have put the engine out of

action, and if you have never tried to sail your boat into or out of harbour - perhaps with the engine running as a safety net - your first attempt at managing without the motor is unlikely to a resounding success.

Sailing in confined waters, often surrounded by moored boats and craft under way, calls for good boat control. To stay clear of trouble you must think like a chess player. The next move may look good for the moment, but if you commit yourself to it, what is going to happen three or four moves along the line?

The jib can be allowed to flap on any point of sailing. However it doesn't do it any good to let it flog in a strong wind.

A sensible combination of sails for entering harbour: a reefed mainsail to reduce power and high clewed headsail for good visibilty ahead.

Controlling speed

The over-riding feature of successful operations under sail is the ability to keep speed down to a level where all potentially hazardous encounters are defused. Many people make the mistake of thinking that the only way to slow down is to ease the sheets. This is true if the wind is forward of the beam. With the wind abaft the beam the mainsail cannot be 'spilled' because it will bring up against the shrouds with the sheet fully eased, still full of wind. In such cases, way can be lost by sheeting the main in tight, stalling the flow of air across it and presenting the smallest possible surface area to the wind. The jib can of course be allowed to flap on any point of sailing.

Oversheeting the main will upset the balance of your helm, but if you cannot bring the wind forward there is only one

other hope of reducing the power of the rig, short of reducing canvas in a hurry. This is to 'scandalise' the mainsail by overhauling the mainsheet, unhooking the kicking strap, then hauling the boom aloft as high as it will go with the topping lift.

Choice of canvas

It is important to get the sail plan right for the job in hand. You must spread enough sail to maintain steerage-way through lulls in the breeze, but not so much that you have an embarrassing amount of power in the gusts, leading to control difficulties. In high-sided river estuaries where frequent strong gusts intersperse with periods of flat calm this makes the choice almost impossible, but if in doubt it is usually better to have too little sail rather than too much. You will do far less damage if you run aground or hit something because you are going too slowly, than if you have just lost control with the boat accelerating towards hull speed. Remember that low-cut genoas are a nuisance in harbours, not only because they usually generate far more power than is the order of the day, but also because they block visibility.

Hoisting and lowering sails

It is axiomatic to all boat handling under sail that on a conventional yacht a headsail can be hoisted, dropped, rolled away, or unrolled to set on any point of sailing. Because they are unaffected by mast, shrouds or spreaders, these vital triangles of canvas can be dealt with no matter which way your vessel is pointing.

This is not the case with a mainsail. While a roll-away main may be removable with the breeze aft, a normal mainsail or mizzen cannot conveniently be hoisted or lowered unless it can blow clear of the shrouds with the wind well forward of the beam. It is certainly not mandatory to come head to wind. This may sometimes be favourable, but a mainsail can be hoisted or dropped perfectly well on a close reach with the headsail drawing and the boat under complete command. Always remember that a head-to-wind boat is a vessel which is on the edge of control.

The fact that a de-powered mainsail is easier to hoist or drop does not mean that the wrath of God will descend upon the hapless sailor who lowers his main with the wind aft. There are times in the life of any cruising yachtsman when to do so will be the lesser of two evils, so when circumstances arise which make it seem sensible, grasp the nettle - top up the boom, sheet in the sail and let go the halyard. One crew member can heave down the luff while another holds the leech aft. It won't be tidy, but in a boat of moderate size or less, it will probably be successful.

SAILING ONTO A MOORING

Many of the principles of picking up a buoy under power apply equally to sailing. The fundamental difference is that while a boat under power has rudimentary 'brakes' by courtesy of her engine running astern, the sailing boat has nothing to take way off but the wind or tidal stream. When sailing onto a buoy it is therefore extremely important to make sure that before you start the manoeuvre you know how you will finally lie to the buoy. Boats on neighbouring moorings will give the most positive clue, but you must ensure that they really are in the same tidal stream as your buoy and that you are not about to be caught out by a local eddy.

As well as observing in which direction the other boats are pointing, note the lead of their buoy lines and how much weight is on them. In a wind against tide situation, boats will sometimes lie head to tide with their buoy lines leading aft, showing that they are actually sailing over their moorings under bare poles.

There are often alternate approaches to a mooring, one apparently easier than the other. The best choice may not always depend on what happens before you arrive at the buoy, but upon the results of failing to pick it up. If one side allows a clearer escape route in the event of things going wrong, always take that option. The majority of damaging collisions among moorings occur after a failed pick-up attempt.

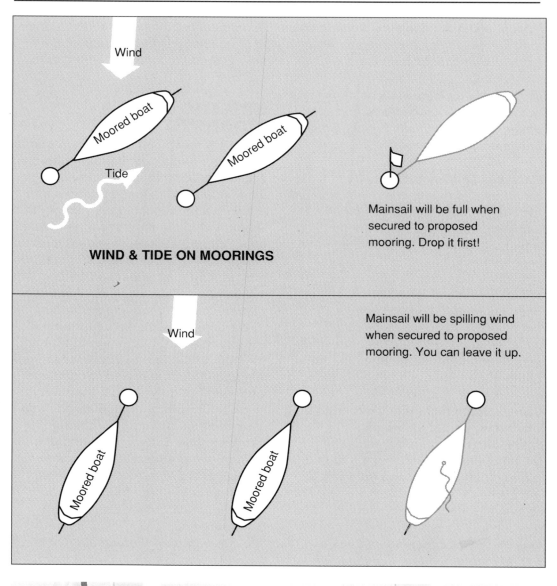

Wind

Moored boat

Tide

Moored boat

Mainsail will be full when
secured to proposed
mooring. Drop it first!

WIND & TIDE ON MOORINGS

Wind

Mainsail will be spilling wind
when secured to proposed
mooring. You can leave it up.

Moored boat

Moored boat

When in doubt, drop the mainsail

The vital question that must be asked before picking up a mooring under sail is, "Bearing in mind the relationship of wind and tide, would my mainsail be able to spill wind if the boat were at rest on the buoy, lying as I expect her to lie?". If the answer is "Yes", then you can approach the buoy with your mainsail hoisted, secure in the knowledge that you can ease sheets to lose way. If the response is either a resounding "No!" or "I'm not sure", there is at least a possibility that the main would fill if you were lying to the mooring. Were this to happen, your boat would be hard to stop in light airs and uncontrollable in a stiff breeze. This situation will arise when the wind is blowing contrary to the tide. If this is the case, or if you suspect that it may be, you must drop your main in good time and make your final approach downwind under headsail only.

Wind across tide, well forward of the beam

The easiest situation occurs when the wind is from a direction that allows you to approach the mooring up-tide on a close reach. You can carry out this pick-up under main alone, unless the stream is so strong that you cannot make headway against it without the drive of the headsail. If you can possibly get rid of the jib, do so. It can be an infernal nuisance to the crew working on the foredeck.

The approach to the buoy should be handled with enough way on to maintain control, but not so fast that you will have difficulty stopping. Use the sheets as accelerators. Sheet in to speed up, ease the sheets to slow down. Pick a transit abeam to give you an indication of how fast you are going, and line the buoy up with something behind it to ensure that you are going in the direction you think you are. Remember that speed through the water will not be the same as speed over the ground.

So long as you are still on a close reach, you will be able to stem the tide sweetly with the buoy alongside one bow or the other, while the foredeck gang pick it up. Remember that the boat is moving through the water, so you should continue to steer into the tide until she is secure. Letting go the helm before the crew has managed to take a turn can give rise to unseemly heaving and grunting, as the yacht slews her keel across the tide.

Coming up to a mooring with wind forward of the beam and across the tide. The jib should be rolled away or dropped as soon as you are sure of fetching the mooring.

Wind against tide

Dropping the main - With wind against tide the stream will nearly always be the stronger influence. The approach will therefore have to be made into it, and your mainsail will have to come down long before you arrive. It is not impossible to lower the mainsail with the wind abaft the beam, but in strong winds it can be difficult. In extreme cases it may even damage the sail. If there is space, it usually pays to come briefly head to wind, or at least up onto a close reach to drop the main in good time. Occasionally there will be no room for this, or perhaps in a strong tide it may be tactically undesirable. In these cases, don't be shy. Top up the boom, sheet in, let go the halyard and pull the sail down carefully by the leech, hauling it aft all the time.

The approach - If the tide is strong and the wind moderate, this is a very simple pick-up to execute. Come in dead up-tide, controlling way with the headsail sheet. Dump it to slow down; sheet it in to speed up. Watch beam transits for speed, line up the buoy as with the wind across tide approach, and you really cannot go wrong. Problems only arise when the wind is stronger and the stream weaker.

Approaching downwind and into the tide, the windage of even a flapping headsail generates a surprising amount of power. If, with the sheet eased right away, the boat is still driving ahead over the tide, your best bet is to lower or furl the sail. Don't be afraid of ditching it too early. If you stop making way over the ground you will have residual steerage-way through the water, and you can always re-hoist part of

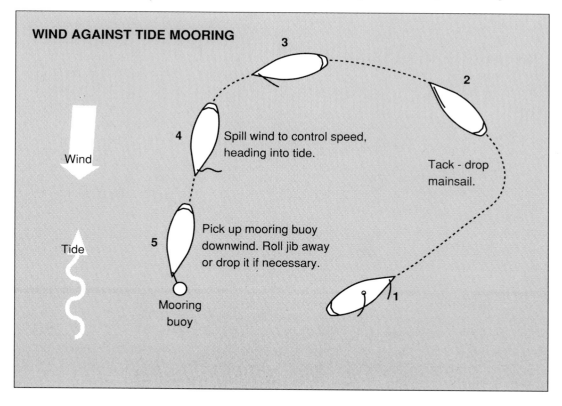

WIND AGAINST TIDE MOORING

3

2

4   Spill wind to control speed,
     heading into tide.

Wind

Tack - drop
mainsail.

Tide

5   Pick up mooring buoy
     downwind. Roll jib away
     or drop it if necessary.

1

Mooring
buoy

the sail, holding out the leech by hand to catch a little air. A roller-furler is ideal for this, as unrolling just the right amount presents no challenge at all.

The most common mistake is to leave the sail set for too long, arriving at the buoy with too much way on. Speeding up is relatively easy, but once you have built up momentum it can be difficult to lose it. One way of working off unwanted speed is to put the rudder hard over, first one way and then the other. The rudder itself has a braking effect; in addition, turning the boat slightly off a dead downwind heading also helps to slow her as she ferry-glides away across the tide.

The stronger the stream in relation the wind, the easier a wind against tide pick-up becomes. With a relatively weak tidal stream and a strong wind it is difficult or in some cases impossible to kill the way completely as you reach the buoy. There is not much you can do about this, other than warn the crew that they will have to be very slick with the pick-up, and must expect to bear considerable weight with the buoy rope.

Slack water

With slack water or wind and tide together you have two choices. You must either pick the buoy up head to wind, luffing up late in your approach to lose the last of your way, or lose all way with the boat stalled on a close reach immediately to windward of the buoy so that she slides across the tide with the mooring on her lee bow. Even if you opt for the latter technique, a last minute luff into the wind is useful to kill any residual way. In either case judgement is required to select the most suitable aiming point for the first part of the approach, which is also the point at which to turn into

wind for the pick up. You may not get this right first time, so you must have a contingency plan for overshooting.

If you think you are losing way too quickly, make an early decision to bear away, go round, and try again. If you leave this too late the boat will stop, and unless you get the headsail aback very quickly you will have no control over the direction in which she bears away. Even if a miracle happens and she does not fall off towards the beautifully varnished boat on the next mooring, there will be a period while she picks up speed when you have little or no control. If you arrive at the buoy still making four knots over the ground, do not try to pick it up; the crew probably won't be able to hold it, but they will succeed in killing your steerage-way. Just take the overshoot and go round again.

It takes both practice and sharp awareness of the prevailing conditions to judge exactly how far your boat will carry her way as you turn her head to wind. Heavy, narrow boats tend to go on further than light, broad ones. Every boat keeps moving for longer in flat water than in a chop. If you are heavily canvassed for the strength of wind, the increased windage will stop you shorter than if you had less sail set, while the rate of the tidal stream is obviously going to affect how far you will move over the ground before coming to a halt. Ideally, you will come in on a close reach across the tide, spilling wind 'to taste' so that you almost arrive at the buoy before you have to luff. This makes the approach easier to judge, because you are trying to hold the boat on a line towards a point only a few yards down-tide of the mooring. Transit this with an immovable object behind it and keep it there. Do not make the mistake of allowing the speed to fall to

When all else fails you can lasso a mooring. Approach with both ends of the line made fast to the boat. Hold the bight, which must be led correctly to the cleats, and when close enough throw the bight over the buoy. Take in the slack as soon as the rope sinks.

the point at which you may lose steerage way. You'll always know when this is about to happen because the boat begins to feel 'spongy' and develops lee helm. As soon as this starts, bear away to regain control, even if it means missing the buoy.

The pick-up

The actual pick-up of a mooring buoy can be more difficult under sail than under power. This is notably so at slack water when with an engine the helmsman can hold the boat stopped for the foredeck crew to slip a line through the ring, while under sail he will not have this luxury. The crew will just have one chance before the boat falls off the wind and gathers way. If there is no pick-up buoy, no ring, or a ring which seems likely to cause problems, it is worth lassoing the buoy as a last resort. Hold a bight of rope over the buoy, then drop or throw it so that it loops round. With luck, the line will sink and catch on the actual riser of the mooring. This lash-up will hold while you rig a proper arrangement. Some skippers seem to treat the lasso as their primary pickup system. This is bad

practice and can lead to disappointment. Always secure properly to the buoy first time if you can. Once you have picked up a mooring and have it secure, stow the sails immediately.

SAILING OFF A MOORING
Wind with tide, or no tide at all

Leaving a mooring under sail needs careful planning, particularly if you are lying head to wind. Ideally, both sails should be set - mainsail first to minimise the time during which the foredeck hands are beaten around the ears by the clew of the jib - so that you have full control as quickly as possible after getting under way. There will nearly always be an easy and a difficult tack on which to make the departure. Often, the latter one is plain impossible. Whatever the circumstances of your departure, the crew can help by walking the buoy aft along the weather side before dropping it.

Sometimes, even the easier tack is fraught with doubts because of another vessel moored close abeam. This is a

Good judgement of wind and tide is needed to reach the buoy at just the right speed for an easy pick-up.

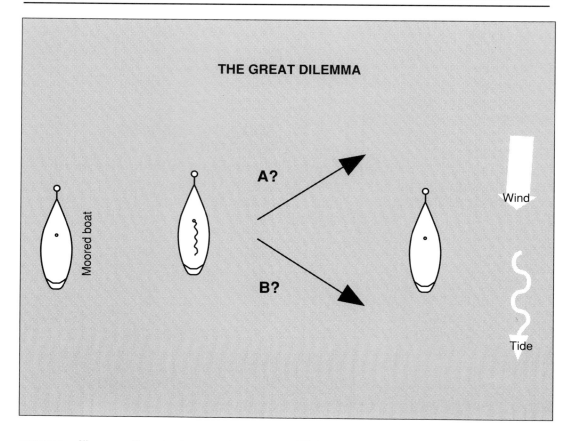

THE GREAT DILEMMA

Moored boat

A?

B?

Wind

Tide

common dilemma, threatening a real danger that you will be unable to weather the other boat, then find yourself unable to bear away quickly enough. Result? A collision. The answer is to examine the situation in the light of these unpleasant possibilities, decide which option will succeed, then operate accordingly. If you are going to windward of the other yacht, do not be in too much of a hurry to sheet in the jib, because until the yacht has gathered full steerage way, this will serve merely to shove her head off towards her victim. If you are trying to bear away, sheet the jib in immediately and ease your mainsheet right out. This will have the yacht spinning off the wind even before the rudder knows she has left the mooring.

Whichever tack you are going for, the basic secret of success is to make sure that you are set firmly on the selected tack before slipping the buoy. If there is a reasonable amount of tide running from ahead you will be able to sheer the boat towards the required side using the rudder, and if in doubt you can make absolutely sure by backing the jib on what is about to become the windward side. Once you have the boat sheered in the required direction, hesitation is fatal. If you allow the boat to start moving that way but hold on to the buoy for a few seconds too long, her bows will be pulled back so she goes head to wind or even right round onto the wrong tack.

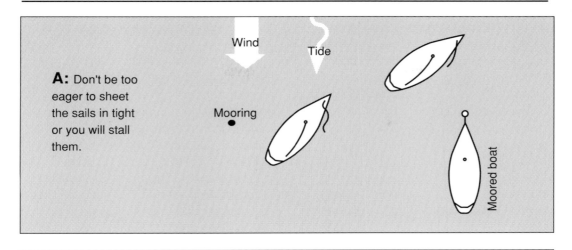

A: Don't be too eager to sheet the sails in tight or you will stall them.

Wind

Tide

Mooring

Moored boat

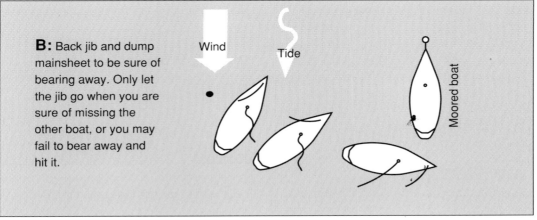

B: Back jib and dump mainsheet to be sure of bearing away. Only let the jib go when you are sure of missing the other boat, or you may fail to bear away and hit it.

Wind

Tide

Moored boat

Wind against tide

With the boat lying head-up to the tide while the breeze blows merrily from abaft the beam, it is imperative that - just as in the pick-up situation - you have nothing to do with your mainsail. That must remain stowed, because if you try to hoist it with the wind abaft the beam, chaos will come upon you. When in doubt, leave it down.

You will therefore depart under headsail only, sail away into clear water, then round up onto a close reach and hoist your mainsail. The inherent danger in this situation is that you will sail between the main buoy and the pick-up, so as to catch

one or the other round the rudder or skeg. If there is a steady breeze and a firm stream running this can be avoided by slipping the buoy before hoisting or unfurling the headsail. Let the boat drop back half a length, then hoist away and sail off. You will have steerage-way all the time, even without any sail hoisted, because your initial speed through the water is the same as the rate of the tidal stream running past the buoy. Even when you start to move backwards over the ground, you will still be carrying enough headway through the water to steer anywhere in a downwind direction. It is often perfectly seamanlike to do this, yet many yachtsmen have an irrational fear of being under way without sail set or their power unit operating. Remember that you can hoist a jib regardless of the wind direction, and a boat will often drift out of a tight spot far less dramatically under bare poles than with a press of sail flogging as it drags her inexorably to leeward.

Whatever your plan for leaving the buoy, once you have hoisted the sails do not hang around dithering. A gust from the wrong direction will fill the sails so that the boat sets off, accelerating until the mooring has been drawn out to the full extent of its scope. The boat will then come to a shuddering halt, and the bow will be dragged round in whatever direction the mooring is pulling it. Your mooring will now be leading in the opposite direction to every other boat in the vicinity, and like as not you will gybe round out of control, straight into your neighbour's gleaming topsides.

ANCHORING

Anchoring under sail is similar to picking up a mooring buoy. The difference is that having dropped the hook, every effort should be made to lay out the cable towards where the boat will finally ride to it. This presents few problems with a reasonable rate of tidal stream running to carry the boat away from her anchor. It is more challenging in a weak stream or at slack water.

As with anchoring under motor, boats too small to use a windlass will have the cable ranged on deck and ready to run in good time. Special care is needed in laying out chain on a gusty day lest you inadvertently range the cable over a lazy sheet, then tack and allow the boat to heel too far. This could tip the lot over the side,

leaving you towing a very long bight of cable.

Do not be too ambitious about trying to drop into a tight berth among other anchored boats. You won't always have enough control to make sure that she runs out her cable cleanly in the required direction. In many anchoring scenarios there is bound to be some random sheering about. If in any doubt at all, leave yourself plenty of space. Getting the boat to lay out her cable may take some time, so do not be in a rush. After the initial drop, let out the cable bit by bit, pausing until there is a definite angle from the vertical before surging more.

Digging in the anchor

While digging in an anchor under power is a repetitive, mechanical skill, doing the same job under sail requires creative thinking.

No Tide - If you come to anchor in a no-stream situation, you will be well advised to drop your headsail before laying the hook, otherwise the head will blow about and the boat will be hard to control. Some yachts will fall back head to wind with the main sheeted amidships, and a reliable person on the helm to keep her head up. Others will not oblige. In small yacht under around 35ft (10m) it is often possible to push the boom out (overhaul the sheet first), and make a sternboard (referred to in Chapter 1) away from the anchor as you lay your cable. This is particularly achievable in a ketch or yawl with the mainsail stowed and the mizzen backed. When the cable has been snubbed, you should have enough way on to let go the boom, and let the boat's momentum carry her on until you feel her stop quite suddenly as the pick digs in.

Wind with tide

More or less the same criteria apply as with no tide, except that as the yacht will be carried more swiftly away from the hook, you have a better chance of success with the main pinned amidships than is the case with no stream running.

Wind against tide

Here, you will be anchoring with the mainsail stowed. Come in under headsail, let go, and see if by spilling wind you can allow the boat to drift back over the ground while still under control. If you can, well and good. Keep letting her drop back as you lay cable. Shortly after you snub, she will come to rest with the tide running past her, indicating that the anchor has set. If the windage of the headsail drags her forward over the tide, drop it and carry on as described. If the hook doesn't bite it will be a simple matter to re-hoist it, heave up the cable, and have a second try.

Weighing anchor

Weighing anchor under sail with wind against tide is an ideal combination, given enough sea room. The boat will be lying head to tide, probably with very little weight on the cable. Haul up the hook and sail away under headsail. Whether you set the headsail before or after weighing the anchor depends on how strong the stream is. If you need some forward drive to lighten the load on the cable set it first; if not, wait until the anchor is on board.

With the boat lying head to wind, particularly if there is some stream from ahead, the situation becomes more interesting. If loads are modest, the crew can heave the yacht up to her anchor,

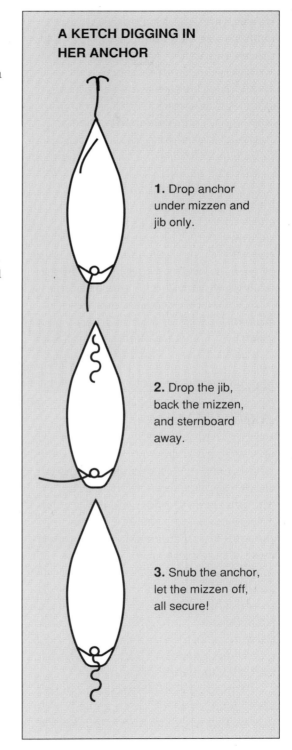

A KETCH DIGGING IN HER ANCHOR

1. Drop anchor under mizzen and jib only.

2. Drop the jib, back the mizzen, and sternboard away.

3. Snub the anchor, let the mizzen off, all secure!

breaking it out as you bear away under mainsail only onto your chosen tack. If this proves impossible, or even hard work, you must give the foredeck hands as much help as you can. Hoist the main, sheet it, and try to tack the boat towards her anchor. The crew should recover cable in shortish lengths while the weight is off it at the start of each tack, then take a turn as soon as the load comes on, recovering a little more each time the boat turns onto a new tack. Eventually the boat will actually sail her anchor out of the ground, so the last stage of recovery should be quick and easy. Care is needed not to build up too much speed, or the cable will start to chafe along the topsides which will do them no good at all.

If you have a windlass, the general system is to decide what sails to set, hoist them, then heave the yacht up to the hook and break it out.

BERTHING ALONGSIDE

The critical elements in sailing out of or into an alongside berth are the ability to recognise the impossible and the strength of mind to avoid attempting it. For example, an approach downwind into a marina berth which is slightly shorter than your boat, with two knots of stream and a Force five behind you, simply cannot be done. If you were tempted to believe that quick crew work with a spring from the amidships cleat will stop her, wise up! You will be doing at least four knots as you arrive at the berth. Even if your crew operate with the speed of light you will either rip out a cleat or part the warp as you carve a deep notch in the marina woodwork, or crunch your stem on the end of the berth.

At the very worst, the tide must turn in six hours, after which entering the berth may be entirely feasible. It is usually only

the conditions of the moment which render a berth unapproachable. These will change in due course. In the old days, men were prepared to wait. Those who would sail their vessels onto quays must think like 19th century mariners, which includes a different sense of time.

Leaving a berth

Leaving an alongside berth with the stream from ahead and an offshore wind is easy. Whether you do it under main only, headsail only, or both, is a matter of whether the wind is forward or aft of the beam and how strong it is. Rig the head and stern lines as slip ropes, and hoist the appropriate sail; headsail with the wind aft, main or both with the wind forward. Slip as appropriate, and go.

With the wind from right ahead or even fine on the outboard bow, leaving under sail is still possible. You will require a stern spring rigged to slip, a stern line to stabilise matters, and a slipped bow line. Hoist the sails and let them and the stream carry the boat back against the spring. Now let go the stern line, back the headsail on the inboard side to swing the bow out of the berth, and slip the bow line. Good fendering on the inboard quarter is important as the bow must have passed well through the wind before you sheet the sails. Then start to gather headway and slip the spring.

A beam wind onto the berth, unless it is little more than a zephyr, makes any attempt at a departure under sail inadvisable. If the stream is strong from ahead and the wind very light you may be able to swing the bow far enough off the berth and use the stream to ferry-glide clear before hoisting sail, but this is pretty sophisticated stuff and it may not work.

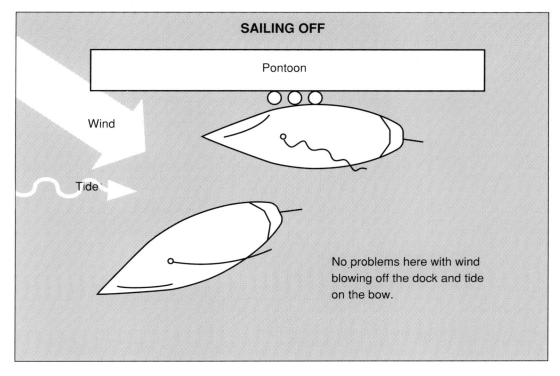

SAILING OFF

Pontoon

Wind

Tide

No problems here with wind blowing off the dock and tide on the bow.

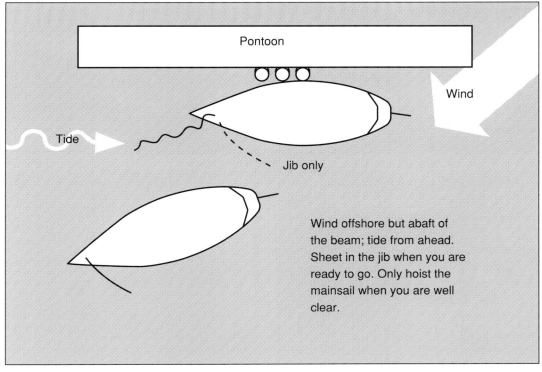

Pontoon

Tide

Wind

Jib only

Wind offshore but abaft of the beam; tide from ahead. Sheet in the jib when you are ready to go. Only hoist the mainsail when you are well clear.

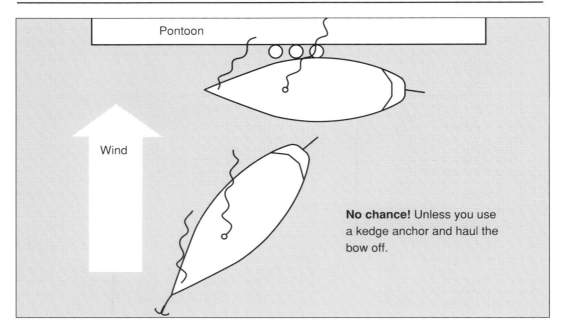

Pontoon

Wind

No chance! Unless you use a kedge anchor and haul the bow off.

With a strong onshore wind and weak stream there is absolutely no chance. The insurmountable problem is that as soon as you sheet the sails the boat will initially move sideways to leeward before she starts to gather headway. This is as inexorable as the forenoon following the morning watch, and there is nothing that anybody can do to change it. Sailing off a lee shore is a non-starter, and your only way of leaving under sail will be to haul off. Either lay an anchor to windward, or find a convenient pile or mooring buoy on which to attach your warp. You may even be able to hook onto the other side of the river, if such are your circumstances. Hauling off is a simple matter, but it is not always convenient and it takes time, the commodity which most of us have ceased to understand.

With the tidal stream from astern you need to have a firm offshore breeze to consider a departure under sail. When leaving a berth under power with the stream from astern the best way out is usually backwards. This is not an option under sail, so the only sensible course of action is to 'wind ship' - turn her round so she is head-up to the stream. If this proves impossible, as it sometimes may with traditional yachts featuring long bowsprits and overhanging booms, departure will have to be made ahead. If there is room, you could try a partial trial run to see if the operation will be feasible. Hoist whatever sail you intend to use, rig head and stern lines as slip ropes, and ease the head line. If the breeze is strong enough to blow the bows off the berth, slip the lines and sail away. If the bow will not blow out far enough, re-secure the lines, lower the sails, bend on a large whisky and wait for the tide to turn.

The most efficient way to wind ship is usually to lead the bow spring out through the bow fairlead to the pontoon abreast the stern or slightly aft of it. Take off all the other lines, except the stern rope. Make sure the inboard side of the bow is well fendered and position your strongest crewman on the pontoon abreast the bow. Slip the stern line, steer in towards the dock, and give the stern a shove. The stream will carry the stern off the berth. As it does so, the strong man on the pontoon starts hauling in on the head spring. The

Winding ship is an old yachting skill which is still very useful today.

boat will tend to nudge onto the berth, so fend off energetically. Keep hauling on the bow spring and let the tidal stream do the work. It should carry her round until she is lying in the berth head up to the stream, with what was the bow spring now acting as the bow line, running to the dock from her outboard side .

Entering a berth

When berthing alongside under sail, the greatest challenge is usually to stop the boat in time. A long clear pontoon or wall is a great help, because if you aim initially for the middle of it, a minor misjudgement is unimportant. You can either secure the yacht at whatever point she comes to rest, or warp her along to wherever you wish to lie. A berth which is little longer than the boat is more difficult, and good judgement of both speed and rate of deceleration are vital to success.

Berthing under engine, with astern power available with which to stop, the approach to the berth could be made fast enough for good directional control. Under sail, you no longer enjoy this luxury since you depend on the influences of wind, stream and a spring from an amidships cleat or a stern line to take the way off. None are as efficient as a burst of power astern on the engine. With tide running, the only possible berths are those which can be approached stemming the stream, unless the wind is very strong and the stream almost negligible. In slack water you will have to find a berth which you enter with the wind blowing from forward of the beam.

The choice of direction of approach, the combination of sails to use, and the control of speed and deceleration are more or less the same as those used for picking

A stern line or 'midships spring' is a vital commodity when sailing alongside. This crew member is surging off the last of her yacht's way.

up a mooring buoy. The essential difference is that with the buoy the direction in which you completed the manoeuvre was dictated by wind and stream, but with an alongside berth you must finish up parallel to it. Finally, in deciding on a sail combination to berth under, always bear in mind that if you sweep the dock with any but the most

diminutive of booms, you may snag yourself, overturn a picnic table, or dismast a passing police car.

Pick your moment and your harbour for teaching yourself more about sailing in tight quarters, but do embrace the opportunity when it is offered. It may seem like bravado initially, but in the end you'll be glad you took the trouble.

6 On the Open Sea

Much of the art that is boat handling takes place in the confines of harbours where the ability to persuade a yacht to turn tightly, stop and go is paramount. Such gyrations are often complicated by tidal stream. Out at sea you are never dealing with objects attached to the ground and tidal movement becomes irrelevant, but there are one or two set-piece manoeuvres whose competent completion mark the good boatman. The first is an essential, which everybody must master. The second, vital to the operator of traditional craft, is still useful for the modern yacht skipper.

MAN OVERBOARD

Losing a person over the side is a rare occurrence. Most skippers manage a lifetime of sailing without gaining first-hand experience of it. However, every year the Coastguard and RNLI statistics show that it remains the most common cause of loss of life from yachts. Care and good harness discipline reduce the risk, but statistics show that it can never be eliminated. Recovery of a man overboard is something that every crew must practise, including rehearsing without the skipper, who has no special immunity against being the casualty.

Most boats have a standard drill to follow if someone goes over the side. It usually starts with the following format:

1. Shout "Man Overboard!" and call everyone out on deck.
2. Throw a lifebuoy towards the casualty.
3. Detail one of the crew to do nothing but watch the casualty and keep pointing towards him.
4. Press the Decca or GPS 'man overboard' button if you have one, bearing in mind that the position given is only good for a short time in a strong tide.
5. Start the recovery manoeuvre.
6. If you have a full crew, have one of your people send out a Mayday message on the VHF in order to scramble the Search & Rescue services. If you are short-handed, you should first make a wholehearted effort to recover the casualty yourself which will save time and reduce the risk of losing touch with him. Should it become clear after a minute or two that you may fail to recover the casualty, call for help even if it means leaving the deck for a moment.

Recovery

Exactly what recovery manoeuvre is chosen depends on the boat, the conditions and the personal preferences of the skipper and crew. There are two common ones, both of which work, and a number of variants which have been devised by individuals to cope with the particular handling characteristics and vagaries of their own boats. The basic manoeuvres are known as 'Quick-Stop' and 'Reach-Tack-Reach'.

Quick-stop recovery

The aim of the quick stop is to keep the boat as close as possible to the casualty.

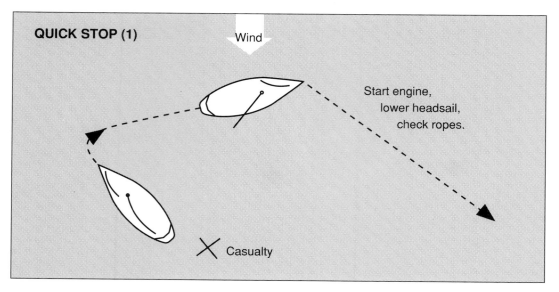

QUICK STOP (1)

Wind

Start engine,
lower headsail,
check ropes.

X Casualty

The helmsman must tack immediately without touching the sheets, so the boat is hove-to.

The first move, which should be carried out immediately, is for the helmsman to tack without touching the sheets, so that the boat is hove-to (this technique is explained further on). At this stage the casualty may be within heaving line range, in which case recovery is an uncomplicated matter of getting a line to him and hauling him back alongside.

If the casualty is out of heaving line range, the next stage is to lower or furl the headsail, check and double check that there are no lines over the side (VERY IMPORTANT!), then start the engine. Sheet the main hard, put the engine ahead and motor to a position directly downwind of the casualty. Approach him head to wind to make the recovery.

This all sounds very simple, so what are the snags? There are several things that can go wrong with quick-stop in practice. Here are some examples:

● The boat is sailing to windward under a large, lightweight genoa which is being carried very close to its upper wind limit.

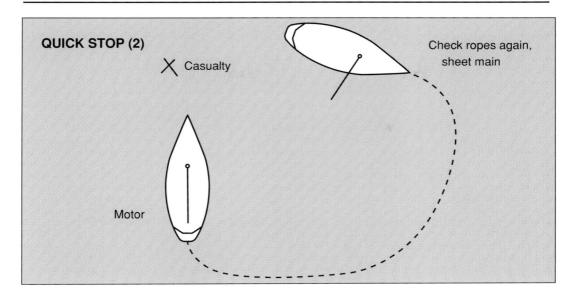

QUICK STOP (2)

X Casualty

Check ropes again, sheet main

Motor

The helmsman tacks without easing the headsail, and the spreader end goes through the sail, catching on the leech line as it does so. The sail cannot be freed or lowered without sending someone aloft to clear it. There is no way out of this one, and it serves to illustrate that any pre-planned routine can fail, given unfortunate circumstances and a little bad luck.

● The boat is running hard under spinnaker. A man goes over the side, the helmsman puts the helm hard down to round up and tack, just as a wave starts to lift her stern. She starts to answer her helm, goes into a violent broach, and is pinned flat on the water with the spinnaker pole sticking up, supporting just enough backed sail to hold her down. Spinnakers really do complicate any emergency situation, but in moderate conditions the quick-stop is perfectly possible with a spinnaker set. If you have not been careful about taping over all the sharp corners of the rig you might recover the spinnaker in two halves,

Approach the casualty head to wind to make the recovery. You can practise as shown with a fender. Just remember that it is considerably lighter and easier to get back on board than a wet, adult body!

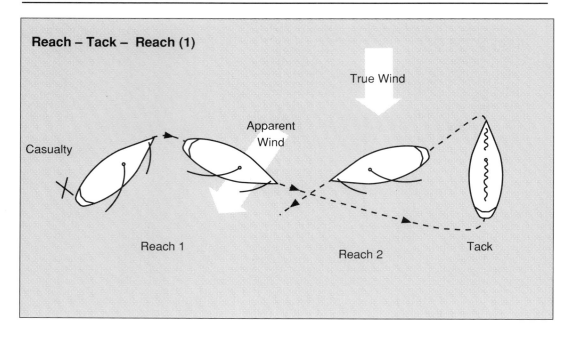

Reach – Tack – Reach (1)

True Wind

Apparent Wind

Casualty

Reach 1

Reach 2

Tack

but that really doesn't matter too much in the context of a life-saving manoeuvre.

● What if having tacked into a hove-to position, the engine will not start? There must be a contingency plan. It can either be to go into the reach-tack-reach routine, or turn downwind, gybe, and complete the recovery under sail. There is a strong argument against gybing during a man overboard recovery if you can possibly avoid it. A gybe can be a violent manoeuvre if it is not carefully controlled. In these circumstances, half the crew may just have been roused from their bunks and not yet be fully alert. The last thing you want is for the incident to turn into a dual recovery, in which the second casualty is unconscious due to the blow from the boom which knocked him overboard.

● What if having lowered the headsail and started the engine, you motor ahead and in spite of careful checks immediately pick up a trailing rope on the propeller? The engine stops with a thud and will be of

no further use. You re-hoist the headsail, only to find that the rope around the prop is the starboard sheet and is so tight that you cannot fully hoist the sail. A sharp knife will solve the immediatiate problem; then a new sheet can be rigged and the recovery carried out under sail. This is a potential problem which you must take the greatest care to avoid. Lives which would almost certainly have been saved, have been lost because of trailing sheets fouling propellers.

The reach-tack-reach recovery

This makes no use of the engine, other than as a back up if things start to go wrong. It is designed to allow the helmsman to sail a simple search pattern, oriented to the wind, from which he will emerge in the best possible place to effect the final recovery. Here is the synopsis of events, once you have gone through the five-point drill outlined above:

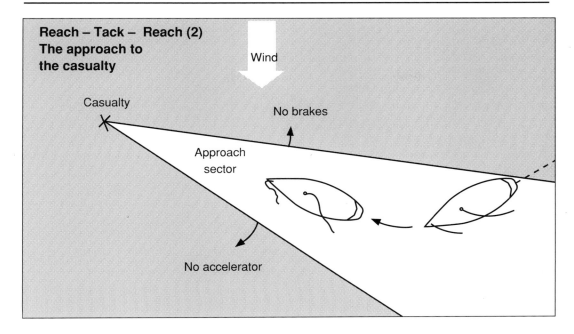

Reach – Tack – Reach (2)
The approach to
the casualty

Wind

Casualty

No brakes

Approach
sector

No accelerator

1. Steer the boat onto an apparent beam reach, so as to place the burgee or wind indicator directly at right angles to the boat's centreline. Since the apparent wind effect has not been taken into account, you will actually be sailing slightly to leeward of a true crosswind course. Sail far enough away from the casualty to give yourself room to manoeuvre, go about as tightly as you are able, and place the yacht on an apparent beam reach on the other tack. The casualty will now be on your weather bow.

2. The next part of the manoeuvre requires judgement. The aim is to approach the casualty on a close reach, so that you can slow right down simply by easing the sheets. There is an arc spreading out from the casualty from within which you should make your approach. If you turn onto your final approach too early you will close him on too broad a reach, and when you ease the sheets you may be unable to spill wind from the mainsail with the result that you

just keep going. Turn too late, and you will not be able to lay the casualty without tacking. If the engine is available it can save the situation should you have misjudged the angle and sagged below the lay-line. A carefully controlled deployment of ahead propulsion will shove you back up to windward and into the approach sector. As with any use of the engine for a man overboard recovery, don't forget to check for lines over the side before you put the machinery into gear.

As the boat slows down in the final stages of her approach, she will start to make more leeway. This will not be a problem if you are picking up on the leeward side. This is generally easier in any case, partly because the geometry of the manoeuvre makes it almost impossible to bring the casualty onto your weather side without a sharp luff at the last moment; but mainly because the freeboard is much lower on the lee side and physical recovery will therefore be easier. In an

Man overboard! Sail on a beam reach on the apparent wind, tack, adjust your return approach as necessary, and then make the final approach for the pick-up.

ideal world it is desirable to lower or furl the jib before starting the final approach, otherwise the flailing sheets can do serious damage to the crew on the leeward side deck who are working to recover the casualty. Don't be in too much of a hurry to get rid of the jib however, until you are sure you will not need its power to drive you up to the person in the water.

What are the drawbacks to this method? The most serious is that it involves putting distance between boat and casualty, and hence increases the risk of losing visual contact. In addition, the initial move which is sailing off on a reach is not ideal for the casualty's morale, since the boat seems to be heading for the horizon at a rate of knots, ignoring him.

How does it work with a spinnaker set? The

bottom line is that success will depend on the crew's ability to douse the spinnaker fast. In theory the quickest means of achieving this is simply to let go the sheet, guy and halyard. None of them should have stopper knots in the end so the sail should simply be blown away. For obvious reasons nobody ever practises this, and a manoeuvre that you haven't practised is always going to be doubtful. If any line snags, you will be in bad trouble. Spinnakers make highly efficient sea anchors, and the last thing you want is to be immobilised until you can find which line has not run and get to it with a knife. It is also possible that you might run over the sail and wrap it round the keel, creating a situation which could take hours to clear.

It is therefore more realistic for most crews to lower the spinnaker under control.

The safest way to do this is to put the boat dead downwind, haul the spinnaker into the lee of the main, run the guy and lower the spinnaker into the cockpit. If all the gear was rigged correctly in the first place, with the windward headsail sheet over the spinnaker boom outside the topping lift, it should be a simple matter to lower the end of the pole onto the deck, leaving you clear to hoist the headsail and manoeuvre in any direction.

The part of any recovery manoeuvre which requires the finest judgement is the final approach to the casualty. This must be fast enough to keep the boat under control, yet sufficiently slow to give the crew a reasonable chance of grabbing him or getting a line to him. A common mistake made with the reach-tack-reach method is to end up with the boat upwind of the casualty, so that stopping for the recovery is impossible. This is particulalrly easy to

do in fractional rigged boats with swept-back spreaders which prevent the mainsail from being eased to more than about 75 degrees off the centreline. With practice, however, even a relatively inexperienced helmsman should be able to make the manoeuvre work, especially if the crew remember that when easing the mainsheet right away has proved inadequate, the mainsail can be further depowered by dumping the kicker.

The Lifesling

There is an item of commercially available equipment which allows an effective recovery without having to make so delicate a final approach. The Lifesling (or Seattle Sling) consists of a strengthened horseshoe lifebuoy on the end of a long length of floating line. It is used by throwing the lifebuoy overboard and towing it. The helmsman circles round the casualty, under

Think about where you will get the casualty back on board. In this case it must be onto the side deck and from there into the cockpit.

sail or power, until the casualty can reach the line. The casualty then works his way along the line to the lifebuoy, and clips himself into it. The helmsman stops the boat by heaving-to if she is under sail, or by stopping the engine if she is under power and the casualty is hauled alongside.

The Lifesling is particularly useful for boats which regularly sail with a small crew. It has the additional advantage that the lifebuoy also acts as a lifting strop, which simplifies the problem of hauling the casualty back on board. It is only effective if the casualty is able to help himself, and will be of no use in the unlikely event of his being knocked unconscious as he went over the side.

Lifting a casualty back on board

Without a Lifesling, lifting the casualty on board can be a problem for a short-handed crew. The first stage is to secure him alongside, which can usually be done by passing a loop of line over his head and shoulders. If there is plenty of wind and he is on the leeward side the freeboard may well be low enough for him to climb or even swim under the guardrails, given suitable assistance. If not, some sort of

lifting device must be extemporised.

The simplest and sometimes the most effective means of helping a reasonably fit person over the rail is to suspend a bight of jibsheet over the side, and have the casualty place his foot in it. As the boat rolls and his weight is eased by his buoyancy, the sheet is shortened by snubbing on a winch. After three or four rolls of the boat, his feet may be high enough for him to climb back aboard.

If the above system fails, you must resort to raising him bodily using winches and tackles. The spinnaker halyard is the best point from which to rig a lifting device, as it is the only halyard which is designed to take load from almost any direction. If you can quickly drop the guardrails in some way (presuming he cannot crawl under), the height of the lift needed can be much reduced.

The most powerful lifting device which can be rigged reasonably quickly is a tackle on the outer end of a halyard, with the hauling part led from the upper block of the tackle, through the headsail sheet lead block, and back to a primary winch. There is enough mechanical advantage in this set-up to allow a 7 stone (45kg) child to lift a 15 stone (95kg) man. The mainsheet reversed would be a suitable tackle, but rigging this can cause all sorts of problems. It is more sensible to carry a dedicated purchase of proper length, all ready to deploy. This may sound prodigal with the ship's funds, but such a tackle will cost considerably less than a dozen new charts.

The only means of ensuring success in any manoeuvre is familiarity through repetition. Skill at bringing a boat alongside improves with experience, because this is something we do every time we go sailing. Recovering a man overboard is an ability which, given bad luck, we might only ever have to do once. It needs a conscious effort to practise, and to work out which is the best plan for you, your boat and your crew. Even if you never have to put your plan to use in a real situation, the fact that you have worked conscientiously on it should allow you to sail with more confidence, secure in the knowledge that you could cope with this accident, should it ever happen.

HEAVING-TO

There are many occasions offshore when a sailor feels the need to stop temporarily. This may come as a result of hours of incessant motion, such as may be experienced sailing to windward. The skipper of a traditional craft may decide to opt for this in a gale, leaving the yacht to look after herself while her crew grab a rest, but aboard any sailing boat it can be useful to slow down, lash the helm and brew up. There may be a tide to wait for to seaward of a river bar, or any number of excellent reasons for taking way off the boat, and the only truly satisfactory method of doing so, regardless of weather conditions, is to heave-to.

A yacht hove-to. The reason is perhaps no more sinsiter than waiting for the traffic to clear.

The theory of heaving-to

When a sloop is hove-to, she is stopped in the water by her foresail being sheeted 'aback' on the windward side. This forces her head 'down' to leeward. The mainsail is left drawing, either closehauled or with an eased sheet, which almost balances the backed jib, pivoting the stern to leeward and the head back up to weather. One sail fights the other with the result that the boat loses way. The equilibrium is completed by the helm, which is lashed so as to try to turn the boat into the wind.

A yacht with a traditional hull form featuring a deep forefoot will maintain herself hove-to with the wind well forward of the beam; indeed, a gaff cutter will normally take up what is virtually a closehauled attitude. Unfortunately, because of their cut-away forward profiles and their Bermudian rigs, more up-to-date hull forms generally heave-to with their bows further off the wind, but by juggling the sheets and tiller they can often be persuaded to improve their act. The boat is balancing around her pivot point, so her attitude can be adjusted more or less to suit the needs of the occasion. If the weather jib sheet is eased, the boat heads up; if the main is eased, she will fall off, 'pushed down' by the power of the headsail.

Some of the more lively recent cruising yachts display the dismal characteristic of actually tacking themselves out of the hove-to mode. Before complaining about this, one should consider the immortal words of Ettore Bugatti who, when W. O. Bentley suggested that his vehicles had poor brakes, responded "I make my motor cars to go, not to stop"! How racing drivers coped with this in the 1930s we cannot say, but the answer for today's yachtsman is to ease the mainsheet. This takes out much of the boat's tendency to head up to the wind, and as a result she will lie more beam-on. You may find this unacceptable in big seas, but it does not affect the worthwhile nature of the technique for giving all hands a break in less extreme weather.

How to heave-to

By far the simplest way to put a yacht into the hove-to state is to tack her, leaving the jibsheet made fast. As the boat falls onto the new tack, she will first try to spin on her heel under the influence of the backed headsail; then, as you push the tiller to leeward or turn the wheel to weather, she will settle in and come to a standstill. You can now lash the tiller or lock the wheel, and go below to dress for dinner.

If you feel your crew could use the exercise, there is nothing to stop you ordering them to winch the jib across to the windward side while the boat is sailing her course. You can then move the helm down as she begins to fall off the wind. She'll heave to effectively enough, but you'll make few friends amongst the crew after so much exertion!

Leeway when hove-to

The amount of leeway made by a hove-to boat varies remarkably according to her type. A long-keel pilot cutter of the Edwardian period, when hove-to in Force 8 in the open sea, makes no leeway at all. Instead, she tracks slowly across the wind at anything from 0.5 to 1.5 knots. A modern short-keeled fast cruiser hove to in Force 5 in calm water will, by contrast, find herself plunging away at about 45 degrees off dead downwind, making up to 2 knots. In a gale, her leeway will be prodigious. If you have a trailing log, you can check the speed of your leeway by streaming this

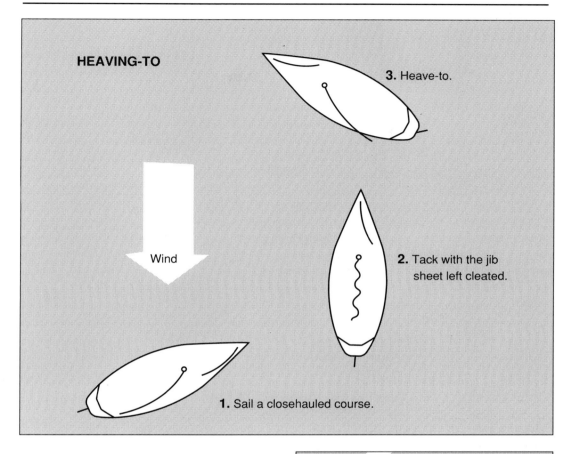

HEAVING-TO

3. Heave-to.

Wind

2. Tack with the jib sheet left cleated.

1. Sail a closehauled course.

invaluable instrument from your weather quarter. It will read distance run accurately. Do not expect similar performance from your through-hull log. This will be in error because the boat is going sideways and so its fixed impeller cannot cope.

Regardless of your log type, the direction of your actual progress through the water can readily be ascertained by sighting along the 'wake slick' with the handbearing compass. The reading is the reciprocal of your actual 'heading'. Add 180 degrees to it, and that is your direction of drift.

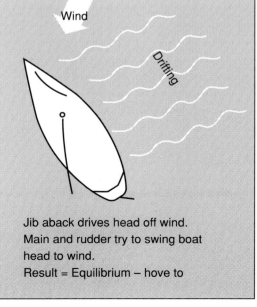

Wind

Drifting

Jib aback drives head off wind.
Main and rudder try to swing boat head to wind.
Result = Equilibrium – hove to

Heaving-to would release the helmsman, and make things easier when reefing the mainsail.

Heaving-to under full sail

To place the truth in a nutshell, heaving-to with a genoa set on a masthead rig is a washout. The sail comes aback against the shrouds or even the spreaders, where it is immediately at risk of damage. Because of its comparatively large area, it will also overpower the mainsail, rendering the desired balance almost unobtainable. The effect of a genoa set on a fractional rig is less drastic, but even so it may prove too much for a satisfactory equilibrium to be achieved.

With either masthead or fractional rigs, the creative use of a roller genoa gives you an ideal opportunity to balance the boat when she is hove-to. In a modern yacht, heaving-to is usually most useful when the boat is already under short sail and you are going for the second or third reef. By then, you may well have a working jib set, under which she should heave-to without difficulty.

Heaving-to for reefing

In practice, heaving-to in order to reef is an ideal arrangement for many yachts. Once she is hove-to, the boat requires no helmsman so an extra person is released to assist at the mast, or to pull down the reef alone if there is no one else on watch. With the traditional hull form, the system worked wonderfully well. Sadly, some modern fin-keelers are so delicately balanced about their centres of lateral resistance that when the mainsheet is eased to pull down the reef, the equilibrium is crucially disturbed and the boat falls right off the wind.

Fore-reaching

When a boat is hove-to, you can begin to make modest way more or less to windward, by progressively easing the jibsheet and bringing the rudder amidships. With the jib clew held on the boat's centreline by both sheets, and the main in a close-reaching attitude, most boats will sail along contentedly, regardless of sea state. Some yachts will perform best like this with the helm left absolutely free. The technique is known as 'fore-reaching'.

A fore-reaching vessel will be going a little slower than when she is flat-out closehauled and will not be pointing quite so high, but the wear and tear on her gear and crew will be dramatically eased. Furthermore, she will not require a helmsman. The benefits should require no preaching.

Other yachting titles from Fernhurst Books

Boat Cuisine *by June Raper*
Boat Engines 3e *by Dick Hewitt*
Bottoms Up *by Robert Watson*
Celestial Navigation *by Tom Cunliffe*
Charter & Flotilla Handbook *by Claire Wilson*
Children Afloat *by Pippa Driscoll*
Coastal & Offshore Navigation *by Tom Cunliffe*
Cruising Crew *by Malcolm McKeag*
Cruising Skipper *by John Mellor*
Electronics Afloat *by Tim Bartlett*
First Aid Afloat *by Dr. Robert Haworth*
Heavy Weather Cruising *by Tom Cunliffe*
Inshore Navigation *by Tom Cunliffe*
Knots & Splices *by Jeff Toghill*
Log Book for Cruising under Sail *by John Mellor*
Marine VHF Operation *by Michael Gale*
Ready About! *by Mike Peyton*
Sail to Freedom *by Bill & June Raper*
Sailing: A Beginner's Manual *by John Driscoll*
Simple Electronic Navigation *by Mik Chinery*
Simple GPS Navigation *by Mik Chinery*
Weather at Sea *by David Houghton*

If you would like a free full-colour brochure please write, phone or fax us:

Fernhurst Books, Duke's Path, High Street, Arundel, West Sussex BN18 9AJ, England

Telephone: 01903 882277   Fax: 01903 882715

The Autobiography